# BTEC Level 3 National Study Skills Guide in Creative Media Production

**Welcome to your Study Skills Guide! You can make it your own – start by adding your personal and course details below...**

Learner's name: _____

BTEC course title: _____

Date started: _____

Mandatory units:

_____

_____

_____

Optional units:

_____

_____

_____

_____

Centre name: _____

Centre address:

_____

_____

_____

Tutor's name: _____

Published by Pearson Education Limited, a company incorporated in England and Wales, having its registered office at Edinburgh Gate, Harlow, Essex, CM20 2JE. Registered company number: 872828

Edexcel is a registered trademark of Edexcel Limited

Text © Pearson Education Limited 2010

First published 2010

13 12

10 9 8 7 6 5

British Library Cataloguing in Publication Data

A catalogue record for this book is available from the British Library

ISBN 978 1 84690 556 8

Typeset and edited by DSM Partnership
Cover design by Visual Philosophy, created by eMC Design
Cover photo/illustration © Image Source Ltd
Printed in Malaysia, CTP-PJB

**Acknowledgements**

The author and publisher would like to thank the following individuals and organisations for permission to reproduce photographs (Key: b-bottom; c-centre; l-left; r-right; t-top):
Alamy Images: Angela Hampton Picture Library 19, Claudia Wiens 10, 66, Claudia Wiens 10, 66; Corbis: 76; iStockphoto: A-Digit 61c, 61b, A-Digit 61c, 61b, 33, 49, 61t, Jamie Carroll 62b, Christopher Joseph G. Suico 62t, John Takai 62c; Pearson Education Ltd: Steve Shott 28, Ian Wedgewood 59.

All other images © Pearson Education.

Every effort has been made to contact copyright holders of material reproduced in this book. Any omissions will be rectified in subsequent printings if notice is given to the publishers.

**Websites**

Go to www.pearsonhotlinks.co.uk to gain access to the relevant website links and information on how they can aid your studies. When you access the site, search for either the title BTEC Level 3 Nationals Study Skills Guide in Creative Media Production or ISBN 9781846905568.

# Contents

**Introduction:** Ten steps to success in your BTEC Level 3 National          5

**Step One:** Understand your course and how it works          9

**Step Two:** Understand how you are assessed and graded          17

**Step Three:** Understand yourself          21

**Step Four:** Use your time wisely          25

**Step Five:** Utilise all your resources          31

**Step Six:** Understand your assessment          35

**Step Seven:** Work productively as a member of a group          67

**Step Eight:** Understand how to research and analyse information          73

**Step Nine:** Make an effective presentation          85

**Step Ten:** Maximise your opportunities and manage your problems          93

**Skills building**          97

**Answers**          107

**Useful terms**          109

# Popular progression pathways

| General qualification | Vocationally related qualification | Applied qualification |
|---|---|---|
| Undergraduate Degree | BTEC Higher National | Foundation Degree |
| GCE AS and A level | BTEC National | Advanced Diploma |

# Ten steps to success in your BTEC Level 3 National

This Study Skills Guide has been written to help you achieve the best result possible on your BTEC Level 3 National course. At the start of a new course you may feel quite excited but also a little apprehensive. Taking a BTEC Level 3 National qualification has many benefits and is a major stepping-stone towards your future career. Using this Study Skills Guide will help you get the most out of your course from the start.

> **TOP TIP**
>
> Use this Study Skills Guide at your own pace. Dip in to find what you need. Look back at it whenever you have a problem or query.

During **induction** sessions at the start of your course, your tutor will explain important information, but it can be difficult to remember everything and that's when you'll find this Study Skills Guide invaluable. Look at it whenever you want to check anything related to your course. It provides all the essential facts you need and has a Useful terms section to explain specialist terms, words and phrases, including some that you will see highlighted in this book in bold type.

This Study Skills Guide covers the skills you'll need to do well in your course – such as managing your time, researching and analysing information, and preparing a presentation.

- Use the **Top tips** to make your life easier as you go.
- Use the **Key points** to help you to stay focused on the essentials.
- Use the **Action points** to check what you need to know or do now.
- Use the **Case studies** to relate information to your chosen sector and vocational area.

- Use the **Activities** to test your knowledge and skills.
- Use the **Useful terms** section to check the meaning of specialist terms.

This Study Skills Guide has been designed to work alongside the Edexcel Student Book for the BTEC Level 3 National in Creative Media Production (Edexcel, 2010). This Student Book includes the main knowledge you'll need, with tips from BTEC experts, Edexcel assignment tips, assessment activities and up-to-date case studies from industry experts, plus handy references to your Study Skills Guide.

This Study Skills Guide is divided into ten steps, each relating to a key aspect of your studies, from understanding assessment to time management to maximising opportunities. Concentrate on getting things right one step at a time. Thousands of learners have achieved BTEC Level 3 National qualifications and are now studying for a degree or building a successful career at work. Using this Study Skills Guide, and believing in your own abilities, will help you achieve your future goals, too.

## Introduction to creative media production

Choosing to study a Level 3 BTEC National in Creative Media Production is an excellent decision to make for many reasons. The media industries employ a huge number of people who undertake a wide range of job roles using an array of different skills and techniques.

You may be studying for a generic Level 3 BTEC National in Media Production, or you may be following one of the specialist pathways. You may be considering just a small part of the media industry, such as working in television, but there are many different career paths in the media, and several specialist pathways on the Level 3 BTEC Nationals in Creative Media Production to cater for different interests.

The specialist pathways available in the Nationals in Creative Media Production are listed below, but you must remember most colleges or centres will only offer a selection of these pathways.

- Television and Film
- Radio
- Sound Recording
- Print-Based Media
- Interactive Media
- Games Development

## Activity:

Why did you select the pathway you did?

In the space below answer the questions about your choice.

| My pathway: |
| --- |
| What were your main reasons for choosing this pathway? |
| What kinds of job roles might your pathway lead to? |
| What kinds of activities will you be undertaking during your time on the course? |
| What are you most looking forward to on your particular BTEC pathway? |

There are many different jobs in the media. Here are some of roles that you might consider if you follow one of the specialist pathways:

- **Television and Film** – camera operator, scriptwriter, director, video editor, sound mixer, graphic designer, researcher, storyboard artist, part of a visual effects team.
- **Radio industry** – presenter, reporter, programme controller, studio manager, broadcast engineer.
- **Sound Recording** – sound technician, live sound engineer, sound editor, re-recording (dubbing) mixer, sound designer, foley editor.
- **Print-Based Media** – journalist, editor, graphic designer, photographer, marketing or PR professional.

- **Interactive Media** – visual designer, client liaison executive, animator, programmer, database specialist.
- **Games Development** – games tester, concept artist, 3D modeller, programmer.

Some roles may exist within several parts of the media. An animator, for example, may work in television and film, interactive media and games.

Although many of these jobs will require you to work as part of a large team, in some cases you may work on your own or as part of a small team, and you be able to take on several roles.

Which of these jobs appeal to you, and why?

## Skills for your sector

Depending on the pathway you are studying, you will develop a wide range of specialist skills while you are completing your Level 3 BTEC National in Creative Media Production. For example, you might develop the skills to use specialist software programs or the skills to communicate your ideas visually by means of sketches and storyboards.

Whichever pathway you study, many jobs in the media industry rely on the use of IT, and so you might choose units to develop your IT skills in:

- interactive media
- film and video editing
- music technology
- digital graphics
- game development.

Some pathways, such as Games Development and Interactive Media, will have more of an IT focus than others.

It is important to remember you are unlikely to be good at everything. Some people may pick up computer skills more quickly than others but feel less confident about putting their ideas on paper in the form of sketches and storyboards. However, it is important that you put in the effort to develop all your skills, especially in those areas where you feel you may be weaker.

Many personal, learning and thinking skills (PLTS) are essential in the media, such as team working, creative thinking and effective participation in presentations and discussions. These are skills all learners will develop regardless of their specialist pathway. There are many general skills that will be important to your future career development.

- **The ability to develop ideas**
When working on a new project within the media industry, whether it is a script for a radio show, a storyboard for a movie or visuals for a website, poster or game character, you will need to be able to come up with and develop a variety of ideas.

- **The ability to work as part of a team**
Teamwork is crucial within many sectors of the media. The team for a television drama will include a director, scriptwriter(s), camera operators and lighting engineers; radio presenters rely on researchers, producers and sound engineers; web designers rely on programmers to make the sites work technically etc.

- **The ability to research information properly**
Research skills are important whether you are researching the content for a website, video or magazine, or you are developing ideas for a new game or magazine and are trying to find out what would interest the target audience.

- **The ability to plan a project properly and to ensure that you meet deadlines**
Deadlines are crucial in the media, whether preparing the launch of a magazine, game

or film, the broadcast of a television or radio show, or an advert. Proper planning is essential not only to make sure that deadlines are met, but to ensure that the work is of good quality and meets the needs of the client.

- **Communication and presentation skills**
Both written and spoken communication skills are important within the media. Many jobs within the media will require you to write content for products such as websites, or scripts for films or animations, or will require you to present proposals to clients or to other people within your organisation.

In the mandatory units you will learn the pre-production skills for the productions you undertake and essential communication skills for the media industry. If you are studying the Diploma or the Extended Diploma, you will also learn about the sector(s) of the media industry relevant to the pathway you are studying, how to research effectively and how to work to a brief in the media industry.

# Step One: Understand your course and how it works

## Case study: Where could the BTEC National in Creative Media Production take you?

Jason, Hari and Charlotte all decide to apply for the Level 3 National in Creative Media Production at their local college but are unsure of which pathway to choose.

Jason has always wanted to work in the film industry, either as a cameraman or a director, so his choice to study the Television and Film pathway is an easy one.

Hari also considers the Television and Film pathway as he likes the idea of film editing, but he doesn't think he would like scriptwriting or camerawork as he prefers to spend most of his time on computers. When he looks at the units available on each of the pathways, he sees that the Interactive Media pathway would allow him to study video production, motion graphics and composing video, web animation and several other computer-based units, so he decides this pathway would be the correct choice for him.

Charlotte enjoys coming up with ideas and meeting new people, skills which would be useful in advertising, but she is unsure which of the media industry sectors she prefers. She likes the look of the marketing and public relations unit on the Print-Based Media pathway, but she notices that the college is also offering this unit on the generic Creative Media

Production course. On this generic pathway, she understands that she can also choose units in commercial production for radio and advertisement production for television, so she decides that the generic Creative Media Production course would be the right choice for her.

After college, all three students hope carry on studying their chosen fields at university. Both Jason and Hari have chosen the option to do the full National Extended Diploma, which should give them enough UCAS points to progress to university. Charlotte decides to do the National Diploma, along with AS/A2 level English, which together should also give her the UCAS points to go to university.

### Reflection point

If you are intending to progress to university, will the Level 3 BTEC National you are studying allow you to gain enough UCAS points to progress to the course of your choice? If not, what else are you studying that will allow you to achieve the right number of UCAS points?

All BTEC Level 3 National qualifications are **vocational** or **work-related**. This means that you gain specific knowledge and understanding relevant to your chosen area. It gives you several advantages when you start work. For example, you will already know quite a lot about your chosen area, which will help you settle down more quickly. If you are already employed, you become more valuable to your employer.

Your BTEC course will prepare you for the work you want to do.

## There are four types of BTEC Level 3 National qualification: Certificates, Subsidiary Diplomas, Diplomas and Extended Diplomas

| | Certificate | Subsidiary Diploma | Diploma | Extended Diploma |
|---|---|---|---|---|
| **Credit** | 30 | 60 | 120 | 180 |
| **Equivalence** | 1 AS level | 1 A level | 2 A levels | 3 A levels |

These qualifications are often described as **nested**. This means that they fit inside each other (rather like Russian dolls) because the same units are common to each qualification – so you can progress from one to another easily by completing more units.

### TOP TIP

The structure of BTEC Level 3 National qualifications means it's easy to progress from one type to another and gain more credits, as well as to specialise in particular areas that interest you.

- Every BTEC Level 3 National qualification has a set number of **mandatory units** that all learners must complete.
- All BTEC Level 3 National qualifications include **optional units** that enable you to study particular areas in more depth.

- Some BTEC Level 3 National qualifications have **specialist pathways**, which may have additional mandatory units. These specialist pathways allow you to follow your career aims more precisely. For example, if you are studying to become an IT practitioner, you can choose pathways in software development, networking, systems support or IT and business.

- On all BTEC courses you are expected to be responsible for your own learning. Obviously your tutor will give you help and guidance when necessary, but you also need to be 'self-starting' and able to use your own initiative. Ideally, you can also assess how well you are doing and make improvements when necessary.

- BTEC Level 3 National grades convert to UCAS points, just like A-levels, but the way you are assessed and graded on a BTEC course is different, as you will see in the next section.

## Key points

- You can study part-time or full-time for your BTEC Level 3 National.

- You can do a Certificate, Subsidiary Diploma, Diploma or Extended Diploma, and progress easily from one to the other.

- You will study both mandatory units and optional units on your course.

- When you have completed your BTEC course you can get a job (or **apprenticeship**), use your qualification to develop your career, and/or continue studying to degree level.

- On all BTEC Level 3 National courses, the majority of your learning is practical and vocationally focused to develop the skills you need for your chosen career.

### Using the Edexcel website to find out about your course

- You can check all the details about your BTEC Level 3 National course on the Edexcel website – go to www.edexcel.com.

- Enter the title of your BTEC Level 3 National qualification in the qualifications finder.

- Now find the specification in the list of documents. This is a long document so don't try to print it. Instead, look at the information on the units you will be studying to see the main topics you will cover.

- Then save the document or bookmark the page so that you can easily refer to it again if you need to.

## Action points

1 By discussing with your tutor and by exploring the Edexcel website, find out the key information about your course and use it to complete the 'Important information' form on the next page. You can refer to this form at any time to refresh your memory about any part of your studies.

a) Check whether you are studying for a BTEC Level 3 Certificate, Subsidiary Diploma, Diploma or Extended Diploma, and find out the number of units you will be studying.

b) Find out the titles of the mandatory units you will be studying.

c) Find out the titles of the optional units and identify the ones offered at your centre.

d) Check the length of your course, and when you will be studying each unit.

e) Identify the optional units you will be taking. On some National courses you will do this at the start, while on others you may make your final decision later.

f) Find out other relevant information about your BTEC Level 3 National qualification. Your centre may have already given you details about the course structure.

g) Ask your tutor to help you to complete section 10 on the form. Depending on your course, you may be developing specific additional or personal skills – such as personal, learning and thinking skills (PLTS) and functional skills – or spending time on work experience, going on visits, or doing other activities linked to your subject area.

h) Talk to your tutor about section 12 on the form as your sources of information will depend on the careers guidance and information at your centre. You may find it useful to exchange ideas with other members of your class.

| IMPORTANT INFORMATION ON MY BTEC LEVEL 3 NATIONAL COURSE | |
| --- | --- |
| 1 | The title of the BTEC Level 3 National qualification I am studying is: |
| 2 | The length of my course is: |
| 3 | The total number of units I will study is: |
| 4 | The number of mandatory units I have to study is: |
| 5 | The titles of these mandatory units and the dates (or terms) when I will study them are: |
| 6 | The main topics I will learn in each mandatory unit include: |

| IMPORTANT INFORMATION ON MY BTEC LEVEL 3 NATIONAL COURSE | |
|---|---|
| 7 | The number of optional units I have to study is: |
| 8 | The titles of the optional units I will study are: |
| 9 | The main topics I will learn in each optional unit include: |
| 10 | Other important aspects of my course are: |
| 11 | After I have achieved my BTEC Level 3 National my options include: |
| 12 | Useful sources of information I can use to find out more about these options include: |

**2** Many learners already have information, contacts or direct experiences that relate to their course. For example, you may have a specific interest or hobby that links to a unit, such as being a St John Ambulance cadet if you are studying Public Services. Think about the relevant sources of information you already have access to and complete the table below.

| MY INFORMATION SOURCES | |
|---|---|
| **Experts I know** | (Who they are, what they know) |
| **My hobbies and interests** | (What they are, what they involve) |
| **My job(s)** | (Past and present work and work experience, and what I did) |
| **Programmes I like to watch** | (What these are, how they relate to my course) |

| | |
|---|---|
| **Magazines and/or books I read** | (What these are, examples of relevant articles) |
| **ICT sources** | (My centre's intranet as well as useful websites) |
| **Other** | (Other sources relevant for my particular course and the topics I will be studying) |

## Activity: Your future options

At the start of a new course it is helpful to think about what options may be available as you consider a future career in creative media production. All assignments on the programme contribute to your final grade, and knowing what you are aiming for will help keep you motivated.

What do you hope to be doing in, say, five years' time and how do you intend to achieve this goal? What practical and technical skills will you need to pick up along the way? What happens if, as you progress with your studies and training, your career aspirations change?

Create a mind map to explore the range of career options available to you in creative media production, and the routes to success. For example, if you wish to become a television producer, you could explore the different routes to working in television. You will find the internet a useful source of information. If you are interested in a career in television, a good starting point is StartinTV.com. Go to page 108 to find out how to access this website.

Use the space on the following page to create your mind map.

## Career options available to me in creative media production

# Step Two: Understand how you are assessed and graded

## Case study: Being self-aware

William has completed two terms on the BTEC National Extended Diploma in Creative Media Production. He has already decided which university course he is aiming to get on. The university's prospectus says he will need 280 UCAS points to secure a place on his preferred course. William has worked out with his tutor that this means he needs to get at least an average of merits in all his assignments.

William looks back at the units he has already completed on his National Extended Diploma.

'During the first two terms of the course we learned a lot of different skills and completed six units. I really like working with computers, and so I did my best work for the computer-based units on digital graphics, web authoring and film and video editing techniques. I got a merit in these three units, and my tutor says I could easily raise my grade for digital graphics to a distinction if I improve the presentation I did for criterion 1 of that unit.

'However, I've currently only got pass grades for the units on research techniques for the media industries, film studies and single-camera techniques. The tutor says that I can easily improve the pass grade for single-camera techniques to a merit by putting some more detail into my production log and including some reflection on the work I produced. My tutor also says that there will be a chance later in the course to improve my grade for research techniques to a merit. I also know what I need to do to improve my grade in film studies. I know the market is very competitive but I'm willing to work hard to get where I want to be.

'If I don't improve the film studies grade, to obtain an average grade of merits I need to improve my grades for research techniques and single-camera techniques units to merits and improve my digital graphics grade to a distinction.'

### Reflection points

Find a university course that you might like to progress to after your BTEC course. How many UCAS points will you need? What overall grade in your BTEC National will you need to achieve?

## Your assessment

This section looks at the importance of your assignments, how they are graded and how this converts into unit points and UCAS points. Unlike A levels, there are no externally-set final exams on a BTEC course. Even if you know this because you already have a BTEC First qualification, you should still read this section, as now you will be working at a different level.

Your learning is assessed by **assignments**, set by your tutors. You will complete these throughout your course, using many different **assessment methods**, such as real-life case studies, **projects** and presentations. Some assignments may be work-based or **time-constrained** – it depends very much on the vocational area you are studying.

Your assignments are based on **learning outcomes** set by Edexcel. These are listed for each unit in your course specification. You must achieve **all** the learning outcomes to pass each unit.

## TOP TIP

Check the learning outcomes for each unit by referring to the course specification – go to www.edexcel.com.

Important skills to help you achieve your grades include:

- researching and analysing information (see page 73)
- using your time effectively (see page 25)
- working co-operatively as a member of a team (see page 67.)

# Your grades, unit points and UCAS points

On a BTEC Level 3 National course, assessments that meet the learning outcomes are graded as pass, merit or distinction. The different grades within each unit are set out by Edexcel as **grading criteria** in a **grading grid**. These criteria identify the **higher-level skills** you must demonstrate

to achieve a higher grade (see also Step Six: Understand your assessment, on page 35).

All your assessment grades earn **unit points**. The total points you get for all your units determines your final qualification grade(s) – pass, merit or distinction. You get:

- one final grade if you are taking a Certificate or Subsidiary Diploma
- two final grades if you are taking a Diploma
- three final grades if you are taking an Extended Diploma.

Your points and overall grade(s) convert to **UCAS points**, which you need to be accepted onto a degree course. For example, if you achieve three final pass grades for your BTEC Level 3 Extended Diploma, you get 120 UCAS Tariff points. If you achieve three final distinction grades, this increases to 360 – equivalent to three GCE A levels.

Please note that all UCAS information was correct at the time of going to print, but we would advise that you check the UCAS website for the most up to date information. See page 108 for how to access their website.

## Case study: Securing a university place

Chris and Shaheeda both want a university place and have worked hard on their BTEC Level 3 Extended Diploma course.

Chris's final score is 226 unit points, which converts to 280 UCAS Tariff points. Shaheeda has a total score of 228 unit points – just two points more – which converts to 320 UCAS points! This is because a score of between 204

and 227 unit points gives 280 UCAS points, whereas a score of 228 to 251 points gives 320 UCAS points.

Shaheeda is delighted because this increases her chances of getting a place on the degree course she wants. Chris is annoyed. He says if he had realised, he would have worked harder on his last assignment to get two more points.

You start to earn points from your first assessment, so you get many benefits from settling in quickly and doing good work from the start. Understanding how **grade boundaries** work also helps you to focus your efforts to get the best possible final grade.

You will be able to discuss your learning experiences, your personal progress and the

achievement of your learning objectives in **individual tutorials** with your tutor. These enable you to monitor your progress and overcome temporary difficulties. You can also talk about any worries you have. Your tutor is one of your most important resources, and a tutorial gives you their undivided attention.

You can talk through any questions or problems in your tutorials.

## Key points

- Your learning is assessed in a variety of ways, such as by assignments, projects and real-life case studies.

- You need to demonstrate specific knowledge and skills to achieve the learning outcomes set by Edexcel. You must achieve all the grading criteria to pass a unit.

- The grading criteria for pass, merit and distinction are shown in a grading grid for the unit. Higher-level skills are needed for higher grades.

- The assessment grades of pass, merit and distinction convert to unit points. The total unit points you receive for the course determine your final overall grade(s) and UCAS points.

**TOP TIP**

It's always tempting to spend longer on work you like doing and are good at, but focusing on improving your weak areas will do more to boost your overall grade(s).

## Action points

1 Find out more about your own course by carrying out this activity.

   a) Find the learning outcomes for the units you are currently studying. Your tutor may have given you these, or you can find them in your course specification – go to www.edexcel.com.

   b) Look at the grading grid for the units and identify the way the requirements change for the higher grades. If there are some unfamiliar words, check these in Step Six of this guide (see page 35 onwards).

   c) If the unit points system still seems complicated, ask your tutor to explain it.

   d) Check the UCAS points you would need for the course or university which interests you.

   e) Design a form you can use to record the unit points you earn throughout your course. Keep this up to date. Regularly check how your points relate to your overall grade(s), based on the grade boundaries for your qualification. Your tutor can give you this information, or you can check it yourself in the course specification.

## Activity: Assessment

Understanding the UCAS points system will help you plan your route into higher education. Your tutors will help you to grasp the key concepts in creative media production and also make the course interesting and enjoyable. The UCAS points you gain should be a fair reflection of your effort, but the result is only part of your challenge.

Sandra is studying the BTEC National Extended Diploma in Creative Media Production and has nearly completed Year 1. The prospectus for her chosen university says Sandra needs 320 UCAS points to secure a place on her preferred course.

- The 320 UCAS points are equal to distinction-distinction-merit (DDM) or 228–251 grade points on a BTEC National Diploma.
- For a full unit (10 credits), a pass is worth 6 points, a merit is worth 12 and a distinction worth 18.
- There are 17 full units (10 credits) and two half units (5 credits) on Sandra's diploma course. At the end of the first year she will have covered nine full units (10 credits).

Sandra has been getting mainly merit grades but is worried this isn't enough.

Can you do the calculations to see what Sandra needs to achieve in year 1 of her National Extended Diploma to be on track for 320 UCAS points at the end of the course?

Remember that to achieve an overall grade in a unit, you must achieve that grade in all the criteria for the unit. If a unit has four criteria and you receive a distinction in criterion 1, a merit for criteria 2 and 3 but only a pass for criterion 4, your overall unit grade will only be a pass. If you are able to improve your work on criterion 4 to a merit, your unit grade will improve to a merit.

**TOP TIPS**

Always ask your tutor if you are able to improve your work on a project, or if you are able to improve a criterion grade through your work in later projects.

# Step Three: Understand yourself

## Case study: Understanding your own choices

Everyone brings a unique set of skills to their BTEC Level 3 National in Creative Media Production.

Sinead is studying for the BTEC Level 3 National in Creative Media Production (Television and Film). She has an outgoing personality and is always full of ideas, which she loves to present to the rest of the class. She is quick to take a leadership role in group work, but sometimes doesn't listen to ideas from other people.

Gurjeet is studying for the BTEC Level 3 National Diploma in Media Production (Interactive Media). He enjoys working on computers and finds it easy to learn to use new programs. He has always done very well in ICT at school and is well organised and conscientious. If he finds something he can't do on a computer, he likes to solve the problem on his own or by using tutorials he finds on the internet. However, he finds it difficult to come up with ideas and is reluctant to share his thoughts with others. He doesn't like working as part of a group, so he sometimes takes a back seat when decisions are made.

Your skills and type of personality may influence your choice of which pathway to follow. For example, Gurjeet has chosen the Interactive Media pathway because he likes working with computers. Your skills will be a valuable asset both to you and to your group whichever pathway you have chosen. However, it is just as important to be aware of any negative personality traits which may hinder your progress.

### Reflection points

Think about your personality and the skills you already have. In what ways have these influenced your choice of the pathway you are following on the BTEC Level 3 National in Creative Media Production?

Self-awareness means understanding how you 'tick'. For example, do you prefer practical activities rather than theory? Do you prefer to draw or sketch an idea, rather than write about it?

Self-awareness is important as it makes you less reliant on other people's opinions and gives you confidence in your own judgement. You can also reflect on your actions to learn from your experiences.

Self-awareness also means knowing your own strengths and weaknesses. Knowing your strengths enables you to feel positive and confident about yourself and your abilities. Knowing your weaknesses means you know the areas you need to develop.

You can analyse yourself by looking at...

## ... your personality and preferences

You may have taken a personality test at your centre. If not, your tutor may recommend one to use, or there are many available online.

Many employers ask job candidates to complete a personality test so that they can match the type of work they are offering to the most suitable people. Although these tests can only give a broad indication of someone's personality, they may help to avoid mismatches, such as hiring someone who is introverted to work in sales.

# ... your skills and abilities

To succeed in your assignments, and to progress in a career, requires a number of skills. Some may be vocationally specific, or professional, skills that you can improve during your course – such as sporting performance on a Sports course. Others are broader skills that are invaluable no matter what you are studying – such as communicating clearly and co-operating with others.

You will work faster and more accurately, and have greater confidence, if you are skilled and proficient. A quick skills check will identify any problem areas.

## TOP TIP

Use the Skills building section on page 97 to identify the skills you need for your course. You'll also find hints and tips for improving any weak areas.

## Key points

- You need certain skills and abilities to get the most out of your BTEC Level 3 National course and to develop your career potential.
- Knowing your strengths and weaknesses is a sign of maturity. It gives you greater confidence in your abilities and enables you to focus on areas for improvement.

## TOP TIP

You will find more help in this guide on developing your skills in using time wisely (Step Four), working as a member of a group (Step Seven), researching and analysing information (Step Eight) and making effective presentations (Step Nine).

## Action points

1 Gain insight into your own personality by ticking **True** or **False** against each of the following statements. Be honest!

|  |  | True | False |
|---|---|---|---|
| a) | If someone annoys me, I can tell them about it without causing offence. |  |  |
| b) | If someone is talking, I often interrupt them to give them my opinion. |  |  |
| c) | I get really stressed if I'm under pressure. |  |  |
| d) | I can sometimes become very emotional and upset on other people's behalf. |  |  |
| e) | I sometimes worry that I can't cope and may make a mess of something. |  |  |
| f) | I am usually keen, enthusiastic and motivated to do well. |  |  |
| g) | I enjoy planning and organising my work. |  |  |
| h) | I find it easy to work and co-operate with other people and take account of their opinions. |  |  |
| i) | I am easily influenced by other people. |  |  |
| j) | I often jump to conclusions and judge people and situations on first impressions. |  |  |
| k) | I prefer to rely on facts and experience rather than following my instincts. |  |  |

Now identify which of the skills and qualities in the box below will be really important in your chosen career.

> **tact   truthfulness   listening skills**
>
> **staying calm under pressure**
>
> **empathy with others   self-confidence**
>
> **initiative   planning and organising**
>
> **working with others   self-assurance**
>
> **objective judgements**

Use your answers to identify areas you should work on to be successful in the future.

**2** As part of the UCAS process, all **higher education** applicants have to write a personal statement. This is different from a CV, which is a summary of achievements that all job applicants prepare. You may have already prepared a CV but not thought about a personal statement. Now is your chance!

Read the information about personal statements in the box. Then answer these questions:

**a)** Explain why personal statements are so important for higher education applicants.

**b)** Why do you think it is important for your personal statement to read well and be error-free?

**c)** Suggest three reasons why you shouldn't copy a pre-written statement you have found online.

**d)** Check the websites you can access from the hotlink given in the box to see what to include in the statement and how to set it out.

**e)** Prepare a bullet point list of ten personal facts. Focus on your strengths and good reasons why you should be given a place on the higher education course of your choice. If possible, discuss your list with your tutor. Then keep it safe, as it will be useful if you need to write a personal statement later.

## Personal statements

This is the information that all higher education applicants have to put in the blank space on their UCAS form. The aim is to sell yourself to admissions tutors. It can be pretty scary, especially if you haven't written anything like it before.

So, where do you start?

First, **never** copy pre-written statements you find online. These are just for guidance. Even worse are websites that offer to write your statement for a fee, and send you a few general, pre-written paragraphs. Forget them all: you can do better!

Imagine you are an admissions tutor with 60 places to offer to 200 applicants. What will you need to read in a personal statement to persuade you to offer the applicant a place?

Most likely, clear explanations about:

- what the applicant can contribute to the course
- why the applicant really wants a place on your course
- what the applicant has done to further his/her own interests in this area, such as voluntary work
- attributes that show this applicant would be a definite bonus – such as innovative ideas, with evidence, eg 'I organised a newsletter which we published every three months …'

A personal statement should be well written, with no grammatical or spelling errors, and organised into clear paragraphs.

For further guidance on personal statements, go to page 108 to find out how to access a number of helpful websites.

## Activity: Preparing your personal statement

Being aware of your skills, and those you need to develop to progress in your chosen field, will be useful when you complete your UCAS application. It could also help you to make a decision if you are unsure which university courses to apply for.

Completing a skills audit will help you prepare your personal statement. You can use the table below to help you, and add to it as you progress through your BTEC Level 3 National in Creative Media Production.

| Current knowledge and skills | Relevance to the university course of my choice (High/Low) |
| --- | --- |
| | |

| Experiences which set you apart from others | Is this directly relevant to your choice of course, or can it be made relevant? |
| --- | --- |
| Examples | |
| I had a short film selected to be screened at the local independent cinema film festival. | Directly relevant to BA(Hons) TV Production |
| I was a volunteer on an Outward Bound course for underprivileged children. | Gained teamwork and interpersonal skills |

# Step Four: Use your time wisely

## Case study: Jake reflects on his organisational skills

'When I first started on the BTEC Level 3 National in Creative Media Production I seemed too busy or too tired in the evenings. I didn't do any homework in the week, but I wasn't worried – I was sure I could catch up at weekends. But I didn't realise quite how much work I would need to do at home.

'Then I got a Saturday job so the work really started to pile up. I missed one deadline and then had to work all night to meet the next one. I was too tired to listen properly in college the next day. My tutor told me it was becoming a problem, so I made a chart of how I spent my time to see where I could fit homework in.

'I was surprised to find how much time I spent chatting to friends on the internet and playing computer games, so I decided to allocate two hours each evening to catch up on college work. Most days I planned a work schedule in the early evening, so I could relax and play games or chat with friends when I finished.

On Wednesdays I play football after college, so I planned in two hours later in the evening, between eight and ten, which gives an hour to relax once I've finished. I give myself Saturdays off but fit in two hours after lunch on Sunday.

'Two hours a night seems just about right. I can fit other activities into the evening, and I find if I try to work for a longer period I get bored and don't produce good work, or I get tired and irritable the following day.'

Follow Jake's lead. Find a time in your day to complete any homework. Stick to it and make it part of your routine

### Reflection point

Is there a time when you will find it easiest to settle down to homework without getting distracted? What is most likely to distract you (friends phoning you, for example)? Can you prevent these distractions?

Most learners have to combine course commitments with other responsibilities such as a job (either full-time or part-time) and family responsibilities. You will also want to see your friends and keep up your hobbies and interests. Juggling these successfully means you need to be able to use your time wisely.

This involves planning what to do and when to do it to prevent panics about unexpected deadlines. As your course progresses, this becomes even more important as your workload may increase

towards the end of a term. In some cases, there could be two or more assignments to complete simultaneously. Although tutors try to avoid clashes of this sort, it is sometimes inevitable.

To cope successfully, you need time-management skills, in particular:

- how to organise your time to be more productive
- how to prioritise tasks
- how to overcome time-wasters.

# Organising your time

- **Use a diary or wall chart.**
  Using a different colour pen for each, enter:
  - your course commitments, such as assignment dates, tutorials, visits
  - important personal commitments, such as sports matches, family birthdays
  - your work commitments.

**TOP TIP**

A diary is useful because you can update it as you go, but a wall chart gives you a better overview of your commitments over several weeks. Keep your diary or chart up to date, and check ahead regularly so that you have prior warning of important dates.

- **Identify how you currently use your time.**
  - Work out how much time you spend at your centre, at work, at home and on social activities.
  - Identify which commitments are vital and which are optional, so you can find extra time if necessary.
- **Plan and schedule future commitments.**
  - Write down any appointments and tasks you must do.
  - Enter assignment review dates and final deadline dates in different colours.
  - This should stop you from arranging a dental appointment on the same morning that you are due to give an important presentation or planning a hectic social life when you have lots of course work to do.

- **Decide your best times for doing course work.**
  - Expect to do most of your course work in your own time.
  - Work at the time of day when you feel at your best.
  - Work regularly, and in relatively short bursts, rather than once or twice a week for very long stretches.
  - If you're a night owl, allow an hour to 'switch off' before you go to bed.
- **Decide where to work.**
  - Choose somewhere you can concentrate without interruption.
  - Make sure there is space for resources you use, such as books or specialist equipment.
  - You also need good lighting and a good – but not too comfortable – chair.
  - If you can't find suitable space at home, check out your local or college library.
- **Assemble the items you need.**
  - Book ahead to get specific books, journals or DVDs from the library.
  - Ensure you have your notes, handouts and assignment brief with you.
  - Use sticky notes to mark important pages in textbooks or folders.

**TOP TIP**

Set yourself a target when you start work, so that you feel positive and productive at the end. Always try to end a session when a task is going well, rather than when you are stuck. Then you will be keener to go back to it the next day. Note down outstanding tasks you need to continue with next time.

- **Plan ahead.**
  - If anything is unclear about an assignment, ask your tutor for an explanation as soon as you can.
  - Break down assignments into manageable chunks, such as find information, decide what to use, create a plan for finished work, write rough draft of first section etc.
  - Work back from deadline dates so that you allow plenty of time to do the work.
  - Always allow more time than you need. It is better to finish early than to run out of time.

**TOP TIP**

If you are working on a task as a group, organise and agree times to work together. Make sure you have somewhere to meet where you can work without disturbing other courses or groups.

- **Be self-disciplined.**
  - Don't put things off because you're not in the mood. Make it easier by doing simple tasks first to get a sense of achievement. Then move on to something harder.
  - Plan regular breaks. If you're working hard, you need a change of activity to recharge your batteries.
  - If you have a serious problem or personal crisis, talk to your personal tutor promptly.

**TOP TIP**

Make sure you know the consequences of missing an assignment deadline, as well as the dispensations and exemptions that can be given if you have an unavoidable and serious problem such as illness (see also page 94).

## How to prioritise tasks

Prioritising means doing the most important and urgent task first. Normally this will be the task or assignment with the closest deadline or the one that will most affect your overall course grades.

One way of prioritising is to group tasks into ABC categories.

| Category A tasks | These must be done now as they are very important and cannot be delayed, such as completing an assignment to be handed in tomorrow. |
|---|---|
| Category B tasks | These are jobs you should do if you have time, because otherwise they will rapidly become Category A, such as getting a book that you need for your next assignment. |
| Category C tasks | These are tasks you should do if you have the time, such as rewriting notes jotted down quickly in a lesson. |

Expect to be flexible. For example, if you need to allow time for information to arrive, then send for this first. If you are working in a team, take into account other people's schedules when you are making arrangements.

## Avoiding time–wasters

Everyone has days when they don't know where the time has gone. It may be because they were constantly interrupted or because things just kept going wrong. Whatever the reason, the end result is that some jobs don't get done.

If this happens to you regularly, you need to take steps to keep on track. Here are some useful tips.

- **Warn people in advance when you will be working.**
  - Ask them to not interrupt you.
  - If you are in a separate room, shut the door. If someone comes in, make it clear you don't want to talk.
  - If that doesn't work, find somewhere else (or some other time) to work.
- **Switch off your mobile, the television and radio, and your iPod/MP3 player.**
  - Don't respond to, or make, calls or texts.
  - If someone rings your home phone, let voicemail answer or ask them to call back later.
- **Be strict with yourself when you are working online.**
  - Don't check your email until you've finished work.
  - Don't get distracted when searching for information.
  - Keep away from social networking sites.
- **Avoid displacement activities.**
  - These are the normally tedious jobs, such as cleaning your computer screen, that suddenly seem far more attractive than working!

**TOP TIP**

Benefits to managing your own time include being less stressed (because you are not reacting to problems or crises), producing better work and having time for a social life.

Talking to friends can occupy a lot of time.

**TOP TIP**

The first step in managing your own time is learning to say 'no' (nicely!) if someone asks you to do something tempting when you should be working.

## Key points

- Being in control of your time allows you to balance your commitments according to their importance and means you won't let anyone down.
- Organising yourself and your time involves knowing how you spend your time now, planning when and where it is best to work, scheduling commitments, and setting sensible timescales to complete your work.
- Knowing how to prioritise means you will schedule work effectively according to its urgency and importance. You will need self-discipline to follow the schedule you have set for yourself.
- Identifying ways in which you may waste time means you can guard against these to achieve your goals more easily.

## Action points

**1** Start planning your time properly.

**a)** Find out how many assignments you will have this term, and when you will get them. Put this information into your diary or planner.

**b)** Update this with your other commitments for the term – both work-/course-related and social. Identify possible clashes and decide how to resolve the problem.

**c)** Identify one major task or assignment you will do soon. Divide it into manageable chunks and decide how long to allow for each chunk, plus some spare time for any problems. If possible, check your ideas with your tutor before you put them into your planner.

**2** How good are you at being responsible for your own learning?

**a)** Fill in this table. Score yourself out of 5 for each area: where 0 is awful and 5 is excellent. Ask a friend or relative to score you as well. See if you can explain any differences.

| | Scoring yourself | Other person's score for you |
|---|---|---|
| **Being punctual** | | |
| **Organisational ability** | | |
| **Tidiness** | | |
| **Working accurately** | | |
| **Finding and correcting own mistakes** | | |
| **Solving problems** | | |
| **Accepting responsibility** | | |
| **Working with details** | | |
| **Planning how to do a job** | | |
| **Using own initiative** | | |
| **Thinking up new ideas** | | |
| **Meeting deadlines** | | |

**b)** Draw up your own action plan for areas where you need to improve. If possible, talk this through at your next **tutorial** (see page 112).

**TOP TIP**

Don't waste time doing things that distract you when studying for this course. In a media business, time costs money.

## Activity: Planning your time

Complete the weekly planner below to schedule time to work on your projects and homework. Don't forget to schedule:

- college lessons
- work commitments
- social commitments (such as clubs or sport)

If you need to discuss work with other learners in your group outside of college, such as when you are filming or discussing ideas, make sure that you find convenient times each week when you all have time available on your schedule to meet up.

| | Morning | Afternoon | Evening |
|---|---|---|---|
| Monday | | | |
| Tuesday | | | |
| Wednesday | | | |
| Thursday | | | |
| Friday | | | |
| Saturday | | | |
| Sunday | | | |

# Step Five: Utilise all your resources

## Case study: Using your resources

Charlotte and Jonathan have both enrolled on BTEC Level 3 Nationals in Creative Media Production. Charlotte is on the Television and Film pathway and Jonathan is on the Games Development pathway. Both have been given a list of equipment they will need for their course.

There are some items on both lists. For example, they will both need notebooks, sketchbooks and drawing equipment, as Charlotte will need to develop storyboards and ideas for films while Jonathan will need to create development sketches for concept art. As they will have to create large computer files (for video projects or 3D animation for games), both will need personal external USB hard drives to back up work created on computer. It is suggested that they use 500 GB USB hard drives, which are USB powered rather than reliant on a power supply.

However, each list also contains some items specific to the pathway that each will be following. Some items on the list are expensive, and the college does not insist that learners buy every item of equipment, but it does stress what resources will be essential for their studies.

The Television and Film list specifies that learners should have access to a video camera. Some students have their own cameras, but Charlotte doesn't. She saves money from her part-time job and asks her parents to contribute towards buying one as a Christmas gift. In the meantime, she shares a camera that her friend has borrowed from her uncle.

The Games Development list suggests that access to several different game platforms will be useful for the computer game platforms and technologies unit. Jonathan has a Wii and a Nintendo DS and his friend Tom has a PS3 and PSP. Another friend, Amir, has an Xbox 360. So the three friends decide to pool their resources, giving them a wide range of platforms to review when they take the unit.

### Reflection points

Think about the main resources you will need for your BTEC Level 3 National in Creative Media Production. What resources do you own? How can you obtain essential equipment you don't have?

## TOP TIPS

You may be able to borrow equipment. Friends or relations may be willing to lend you equipment or reference books that they no longer need.

Your resources are all the things that can help you to be successful in your BTEC Level 3 National qualification, from your favourite website to your **study buddy** (see page 112) who collects handouts for you if you miss a class.

Your centre will provide essential resources, such as a library with appropriate books and electronic reference sources, the computer network and internet access. You will have to provide basic resources such as pens, pencils and file folders yourself. If you have to buy your own textbooks, look after them carefully so you can sell them on at the end of your course.

Here is a list of resources, with tips for getting the best out of them.

- **Course information**. This includes your course specification, this Study Skills Guide and all information on the Edexcel website relating to your BTEC Level 3 National course. Course information from your centre will include term dates, assignment dates and your timetable. Keep everything safely so you can refer to it whenever you need to clarify something.
- **Course materials**. These include course handouts, printouts, your own notes, and textbooks. Put handouts into an A4 folder as soon as you get them. Use a separate folder for each unit you study.

**TOP TIP**

Filing notes and handouts promptly means they don't get lost and will stay clean and uncrumpled, and you won't waste time looking for them.

- **Stationery**. You need pens and pencils, a notepad, a hole puncher, a stapler and sets of dividers. Dividers should be clearly labelled to help you store and quickly find notes, printouts and handouts. Your notes should be headed and dated, and those from your own research must also include your source (see Step Eight, page 73 onwards.)
- **People**. Your tutors, specialist staff at college, classmates, your employer and work colleagues, and your relatives and friends are all valuable resources. Many will have particular skills, or work in the vocational area that you are studying. Talking to other learners can help to clarify issues that there may not have been time to discuss fully in class.

A **study buddy** is another useful resource as they can make notes and collect handouts if you miss a session. (Remember to return the favour when they are away.)

Always be polite when you are asking people for information. Prepare the questions first and remember that you are asking for help, not trying to get them to do the work for you! If you are interviewing someone for an assignment or project, good preparations are vital. (See Step Eight, page 73 onwards.)

If someone who did the course before you offers help, be careful. It is likely the course requirements will have changed. Never be tempted to copy their assignments (or someone else's). This is **plagiarism** – a deadly sin in the educational world (see also Step Six, page 35.)

**TOP TIP**

A positive attitude, an enquiring mind and the ability to focus on what is important will have a major impact on your final result.

## Key points

- Resources help you to achieve your qualification. Find out what resources you have available to you, and use them wisely.
- Have your own stationery items.
- Know how to use central facilities and resources such as the library, learning resource centres and your computer network. Always keep to the policy on IT use in your centre.
- People are a key resource – school or college staff, work colleagues, members of your class, friends, family and people who are experts in their field.

## Action points

**1 a)** List the resources you will need to complete your course successfully. Identify which ones will be provided by your school or college, and which you need to supply yourself.

**b)** Go through your list again and identify the resources you already have (or know how to access) and those you don't.

**c)** Compare your list with a friend's and decide how to obtain and access the resources you need. Add any items to your list that you forgot.

**d)** List the items you still need to get and set a target date for doing this.

**2** 'Study buddy' schemes operate in many centres. Find out if this applies to your own centre and how you can make the best use of it.

In some you can choose your study buddy, in others people are paired up by their tutor.
- Being a study buddy might mean just collecting handouts when the other person is absent, and giving them important news.
- It may also mean studying together and meeting (or keeping contact by phone or email) to exchange ideas and share resources.

With a study buddy you can share resources and stay on top of the course if you're ever away.

## Activity: Using resources

Use the grid below to list the people you know who might be useful to your studies and how they might help you.

| Person/group | How they could help your studies |
|---|---|
| | |
| | |
| | |
| | |
| | |
| | |

**TOP TIP**

People are sometimes your most useful resources. A study buddy can collect notes if you miss a class, friends can share equipment such as cameras, a local group or organisation (such as a hospital radio station) or a contact in the media industry may be willing to provide work experience.

# Step Six: Understand your assessment

## Case study: Gaining the marks you need

Jason is taking a BTEC Level 3 National Diploma in Creative Media Production. He has just received feedback on his first assignment.

'My first assignment was completed last week and ever since I handed it in I have been a bit anxious about how I have done. In today's lesson we were each given an assessment feedback sheet for the assignment. It is much more detailed than I had expected. The comments are linked to the grading criteria and unit content, which really helps me understand how the work could be improved.

'The assignment covered grading criterion 2 of Unit 7: Understanding the Creative Media Sector. We had to research job roles and employment opportunities in one of the sectors of the media.

'I looked at the radio industry and found out about different roles such as presenter, reporter, programme controller, studio manager and broadcast engineer. I looked at the skills and training necessary to gain employment in each role, and at examples of how the jobs in the radio industry are advertised.

'The assessment feedback sheet covers what I had done well as well as giving advice on how to improve the work. The tutor said that I had included enough detail in my assignment work to achieve a pass, but that if I add some more information about the sort of skills and professional behaviour required in the jobs that I researched and give some more detailed examples, then I can hopefully get a merit for this part of the unit.'

### Reflection points

What opportunities do you think there are for Jason to improve his grades for this assignment? What would you advise him to do to make these improvements?

---

Being successful on any BTEC Level 3 National course means first understanding what you must do in your assignments – and then doing it.

Your assignments focus on topics you have already covered in class. If you've attended regularly, you should be able to complete them confidently.

However, there are some common pitfalls it's worth thinking about. Here are tips to avoid them:

- Read the instructions (the assignment brief) properly and several times before you start.

- Make sure you understand what you are supposed to do. Ask if anything is unclear.

- Complete every part of a task. If you ignore a question, you can't meet the grading criteria.

- Prepare properly. Do your research or reading before you start. Don't guess the answers.

- Communicate your ideas clearly. You can check this by asking someone who doesn't know the subject to look at your work.

- Only include relevant information. Padding out answers makes it look as if you don't know your subject.

- Do the work earlier rather than later to avoid any last-minute panics.

- Pay attention to advice and feedback that your tutor has given you.

## The assignment 'brief'

This may be longer than its name implies! The assignment brief includes all the instructions for an assignment and several other details, as you can see in the table below.

| What will you find in a BTEC Level 3 National assignment brief? | |
|---|---|
| **Content** | **Details** |
| Title | This will link to the unit and learning outcomes |
| Format/style | Written assignment, presentation, demonstration etc |
| Preparation | Read case study, do research etc |
| Learning outcomes | These state the knowledge you must demonstrate to obtain a required grade |
| Grading criterion/ criteria covered | For example, P1, M1, D1 |
| Individual/group work | Remember to identify your own contribution in any group work |
| Feedback | Tutor, peer review |
| Interim review dates | Dates to see your tutor |
| Final deadline | Last submission date |

## Your centre's rules and regulations

Your centre will have several policies and guidelines about assignments, which you need to check carefully. Many, such as those listed below, relate to Edexcel policies and guidelines.

- The procedure to follow if you have a serious problem and can't meet a deadline. An extension may be granted.
- The penalty for missing a deadline without good reason.
- The penalty for copying someone else's work. This is usually severe, so never share your work (or CDs or USB flash drive) with anyone else, and don't borrow theirs.
- **Plagiarism** is also serious misconduct. This means copying someone's work or quoting from books and websites and pretending it is your own work.
- The procedure to follow if you disagree with the grade you are given.

## Understanding the question or task

There are two aspects to a question or task. The first is the **command words**, which are described below. The second is the **presentation instructions**, which is what you are asked to do – don't write a report when you should be producing a chart!

Command words, such as 'explain', 'describe', 'analyse', 'evaluate' state how a question must be answered. You may be asked to 'describe' something at pass level, but you will need to do more, perhaps 'analyse' or 'evaluate', to achieve merit or distinction.

Many learners fail to achieve higher grades because they don't realise the difference between these words. Instead of analysing or evaluating they give an explanation instead. Adding more details won't achieve a higher grade – you need to change your whole approach to the answer.

The **grading grid** for each unit of your course gives you the command words, so that you know what to do to achieve a pass, merit or distinction. The tables that follow show you what is usually required when you see a particular command word. These are just examples to guide you, as the exact response will depend on the question. If you have any doubts, check with your tutor before you start work.

There are two important points to note.

- A command word, such as 'create' or 'explain', may be repeated in the grading criteria for different grades. In these cases the complexity or range of the task itself increases at the higher grades.
- Command words vary depending on your vocational area. So Art and Design grading grids may use different command words from Applied Science, for example.

## To obtain a pass grade

To achieve a pass you must usually demonstrate that you understand the important facts relating to a topic and can state these clearly and concisely.

| Command words for a pass | Meaning |
|---|---|
| Create (or produce) | Make, invent or construct an item. |
| Describe | Give a clear, straightforward description that includes all the main points and links these together logically. |
| Define | Clearly explain what a particular term means and give an example, if appropriate, to show what you mean. |
| Explain … how/why | Set out in detail the meaning of something, with reasons. It is often helpful to give an example of what you mean. Start with the topic then give the 'how' or 'why'. |
| Identify | Distinguish and state the main features or basic facts relating to a topic. |
| Interpret | Define or explain the meaning of something. |
| Illustrate | Give examples to show what you mean. |
| List | Provide the information required in a list rather than in continuous writing. |
| Outline | Write a clear description that includes all the main points but avoid going into too much detail. |
| Plan (or devise) | Work out and explain how you would carry out a task or activity. |
| Select (and present) information | Identify relevant information to support the argument you are making and communicate this in an appropriate way. |
| State | Write a clear and full account. |
| Undertake | Carry out a specific activity. |
| Examples: | |
| Identify the main features on a digital camera. | |
| Outline the steps to take to carry out research for an assignment. | |

## To obtain a merit grade

To obtain a merit you must prove that you can apply your knowledge in a specific way.

| Command words for a merit | Meaning |
|---|---|
| Analyse | Identify separate factors and say how they relate to each other and how each one relates to the topic. |
| Classify | Sort your information into appropriate categories before presenting or explaining it. |
| Compare and contrast | Identify the main factors that apply in two or more situations and explain the similarities and differences or advantages and disadvantages. |
| Demonstrate | Provide several relevant examples or appropriate evidence which support the arguments you are making. In some vocational areas this may also mean giving a practical performance. |
| Discuss | Provide a thoughtful and logical argument to support the case you are making. |
| Explain (in detail) | Provide details and give reasons and/or evidence to clearly support the argument you are making. |
| Implement | Put into practice or operation. You may also have to interpret or justify the effect or result. |
| Interpret | Understand and explain an effect or result. |
| Justify | Give appropriate reasons to support your opinion or views, and show how you arrived at these conclusions. |
| Relate/report | Give a full account, with reasons. |
| Research | Carry out a full investigation. |
| Specify | Provide full details and descriptions of selected items or activities. |
| Examples: | |

Examples:

Compare and contrast the performance of two different digital cameras.

Explain in detail the steps to take to research an assignment.

## To obtain a distinction grade

To obtain a distinction you must prove that you can make a reasoned judgement based on appropriate evidence.

| Command words for a distinction | Meaning |
| --- | --- |
| Analyse | Identify the key factors, show how they are linked, and explain the importance and relevance of each. |
| Assess | Give careful consideration to all the factors or events that apply, and identify which are the most important and relevant, with reasons. |
| Comprehensively explain | Give a very detailed explanation that covers all the relevant points, and give reasons for your views or actions. |
| Critically comment | Give your view after you have considered all the evidence, particularly the importance of both the relevant positive and negative aspects. |
| Evaluate | Review the information and then bring it together to form a conclusion. Give evidence to support each of your views or statements. |
| Evaluate critically | Review the information to decide the degree to which something is true, important or valuable. Then assess possible alternatives, taking into account their strengths and weaknesses if they were applied instead. Then give a precise and detailed account to explain your opinion. |
| Summarise | Identify/review the main, relevant factors and/or arguments so that these are explained in a clear and concise manner. |

Examples:

Assess ten features commonly found on a digital camera.

Analyse your own ability to carry out effective research for an assignment.

**TOP TIP**

Check that you understand exactly how you need to demonstrate each of the learning outcomes specified in the assignment.

## Responding positively

Assignments enable you to demonstrate what you know and how you can apply it. You should respond positively to the challenge and give it your best shot. Being well organised and having confidence in your own abilities helps too, and this is covered in the next section.

### Key points

- Read instructions carefully so that you don't make mistakes that can easily be avoided, such as only doing part of the set task.

- Note the assignment deadline on your planner and any interim review dates. Schedule work around these dates to make the most of reviews with your tutor.

- Check your centre's policies relating to assignments, such as how to obtain an extension or query a final grade.

- Expect command words and/or the complexity of a task to be different at higher grades, because you have to demonstrate higher-level skills.

**TOP TIP**

All your assignments will relate to topics you have covered and work you have done in class. They're not meant to be a test to catch you out.

### Action points

1 Check your ability to differentiate between different types of command words by doing this activity.
  a) Prepare a brief description of your usual lifestyle (pass level).
  b) Describe and justify your current lifestyle (merit level).
  c) Critically evaluate your current lifestyle (distinction level).

It would be a good idea to check that your answer is accurate and appropriate by showing it to your tutor at your next tutorial.

**TOP TIP**

When presenting evidence for an assessment, think about the person who will be looking through it. Plan your 'pitch' well and make it easy for the assessor to match your evidence against the grading criteria.

# Sample assignment

**Note about assignments**
All learners are different and will approach their assignments in different ways. The sample assignment that follows shows how one learner answered a brief to achieve pass, merit and distinction level criteria. This learner work shows just one way in which these grading criteria can be evidenced. There are no standard or set answers. If you produce the required evidence for each task, then you will achieve the grading criteria covered by the assignment.

## Front sheet

Check the front sheet of your assignment carefully and ensure you complete all necessary fields, eg your name.

Make a note of when the work for the assignment is due and be sure that you know your school or college's policy on meeting deadlines.

Before submitting your work it is useful to run it past your tutor for comment. There may be essential evidence which you have missed.

When compiling evidence, do check that it meets the requirements of the grading criterion. Evidence could be a written report, class presentation, audiovisual presentation, information you have commented upon, or even a website.

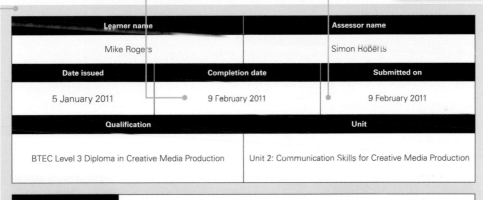

| Learner name | | Assessor name | |
|---|---|---|---|
| Mike Rogers | | Simon Roberts | |
| **Date issued** | **Completion date** | | **Submitted on** |
| 5 January 2011 | 9 February 2011 | | 9 February 2011 |
| **Qualification** | | **Unit** | |
| BTEC Level 3 Diploma in Creative Media Production | | Unit 2: Communication Skills for Creative Media Production | |

| Assignment title | Create your own magazine |
|---|---|

In this assessment you will have opportunities to provide evidence against the following criteria.
Indicate the page numbers where the evidence can be found.

| Criteria reference | To achieve the criteria the evidence must show that the learner is able to: | Task no. | Evidence |
|---|---|---|---|
| P1 | use appropriate techniques to extract relevant information from written sources | 1 | a) Research plan and summary of information extracted |
| M1 | use appropriate techniques to extract information from written sources with some precision | | |
| D1 | use appropriate techniques to extract comprehensive information from written sources | | (pages 1–6) |
| P2 | present a media production report which conveys relevant information | 1, 2 | a) Research plan |
| | | | b) Draft proposal |
| M2 | present a structured and detailed media production report which conveys information and explains conclusions with clarity | | c) Final proposal |
| D2 | present a well-structured and substantial media production report which conveys information with precise exemplification and justifies conclusions with supporting arguments | | d) Draft treatment |
| | | | e) Final treatment |

This grid is very important as it shows how your work will be graded for each of the criteria. Remember that to achieve a pass, merit or distinction overall, you must achieve at least that grade in ALL of the criteria.

In this area you can list exactly what evidence you are submitting to meet each criterion.

| P3 | review reports to make changes with occasional beneficial effects | 2 | b) Draft proposal |
| M3 | review reports to make changes with frequent beneficial effects | | c) Final proposal |
| D3 | review reports to make changes with consistently beneficial effects | | d) Draft treatment |
| | | | e) Final treatment |
| P4 | deploy and manage appropriate technology to pitch a media production proposal | 3 | f) Notes for my pitch |
| M4 | deploy and manage technology to pitch a media production proposal effectively and with some imagination | | g) Script |
| D4 | deploy and manage technology to pitch a media production proposal with creativity and flair and to near-professional standards | | h) PowerPoint presentation |
| P5 | employ appropriate forms of address in a media production pitch to communicate ideas | 3 | f) Notes for my pitch |
| M5 | employ forms of address in a media production pitch to communicate ideas effectively | | g) Script |
| D5 | employ forms of address in a media production pitch with flair to communicate ideas with impact | | h) PowerPoint presentation |
| | | | i) Tutor observation record |

**Learner declaration**

I certify that the work submitted for this assignment is my own and research sources are fully acknowledged.

Learner signature:  *Mike Rogers*                     Date: *9 February 2011*

Make sure that any evidence you present is your own and not copied or cut and pasted from other people's work. If you use quotes from other reference sources make sure these are clearly referenced in the text and in a bibliography at the end of your submission.

# Assignment brief

Scenarios are intended to help you relate the assignment tasks to the kind of things you may be asked to produce in the media industry, and to think about what would be required from you working for a real company or client.

Always keep the assignment title in mind when producing work for your assessment. This will help ensure you produce work appropriate to the topic.

| Unit title | Unit 2: Communication Skills for Creative Media Production |
|---|---|
| Qualification | BTEC Level 3 Diploma in Creative Media Production |
| Start date | 5 January 2011 |
| Interim deadline | 2 February 2011 |
| Deadline date | 9 February 2011 |
| Assessor | Simon Roberts |

| Assignment title | Create your own magazine |
|---|---|

**The purpose of this assignment is to.**
use communication skills in planning, proposing and pitching an idea for a media production.

**Scenario**
You have been commissioned by a publishing company to come up with ideas for a new magazine for the teen market. The company is interested in broad appeal but also realises that there may be some niche areas of interest that have yet to be exploited that might become the next big thing.

You will need to come up with a feasible idea and conduct some detailed research, before preparing a proposal and treatment and, finally, pitching your idea to the publishing company.

**Task 1**
Generate initial ideas for your magazine and conduct research into their viability. To do this, first draft a research plan to outline possible sources of information that will help you to develop your magazine idea.

Next, look at different sources of information (for example, the internet, books and similar magazines that are currently available) to gain a better understanding of the teen magazine market and patterns of consumption. Show how and where you have extracted information from these sources by annotating your work and producing a report that summarises.
- the sources you used to find information
- the information you extracted from each source
- how and why the information was relevant
- how you will use the information to create your final product.

Be sure to write a final conclusion detailing how relevant you found the whole process and be sure that you have included a range of sources. The information you gather must be targeted and relevant to your ideas and will form the basis of your proposal and treatment (Task 2) which you will present to the publishing company.

**This provides evidence for P1, M1, D1 and P2, M2, D2**

**Task 2**
Now that you have conducted your research and have an idea for your new magazine it is time to create your proposal and treatment.

1. Write up your proposal using a relevant format and introduce/convey your ideas for the new magazine. Be sure to include details of how you arrived at this idea and reference your research findings to support your comments.

2. Review that proposal, noting changes and improvements that could make it more detailed and ready to be drafted into a treatment. Be sure to check your grammar and spelling.

3. Using the notes you have made for proposed changes, draft a treatment that provides a more detailed account of your product, its contents, style, format, layout, target audience, distribution and intentions. You will need to check your treatment to eradicate errors and ensure clarity of expression.

**This provides evidence for: P2, M2, D2 and P3, M3, D3**

Where tasks cover multiple criteria, try to understand which elements go towards which of the criteria. In task 2 presenting the report goes towards criterion 2, and reviewing it to make changes goes towards criterion 3.

Where tasks cover multiple criteria, try to understand which elements go towards which of the criteria. In task 1 showing how you have extracted the information goes towards criterion 1, and presenting the report goes towards criterion 2.

These books and websites may prove useful in helping you prepare your reports and presentations.

**Task 3**

Once your treatment has been approved and signed off by your tutor you will need to prepare a presentation to pitch your idea to the publishing company.

1 You will need to select an appropriate format to present your ideas, and you must include all relevant information from your treatment, as well as adding creative touches such as links and animations.

2 You may also wish to produce a handout for the audience that outlines the ideas in your presentation.

3 You will need to prepare a script or some cue cards to use during the presentation to ensure that you know what you are saying and when.

4 During the presentation you must present your concept to the client clearly and persuasively in order to convince them to commission your idea.

5 At the end of the pitch you must hand in all copies of your work to your tutor for assessment.

**This provides evidence for P4, M4, D4 and P5, M5, D5**

**Final assignment evidence**
- Research plan
- Copies of information you have gathered, with annotations
- Report detailing extracted information.
- Completed and draft versions of the proposal and treatment showing the process of review and the improvements made to both documents.
- Tutor observation record for the pitch (a video recording of the pitch could also be provided).
- Presentation materials, including handouts (if used), scripts/cue cards.

**Sources of information**

**Books**

Bradbury, A. – *Successful Presentation Skills*, 3rd edition (Kogan Page, 2006) 9780749445607
Condrill, J. and Bough, B. – *101 Ways to Improve Your Communication Skills Instantly* (GoalMinds Inc, 1999) 9780966141498
Cottrel, S. – *Critical Thinking Skills: Developing Effective Analysis and Argument* (Palgrave Macmillan, 2005) 9781403996855
Hargie, O. – *The Handbook of Communication Skills*, 2nd edition (Routledge, 1997) 9780415123266)
Mikulecky, B. and Jeffries, L. – *More Reading Power: Reading for Pleasure, Comprehension Skills, Thinking Skills, Reading Faster* (Pearson, 2003) 9780130611994

**Websites**

www.mindtools.com: free online tools that help you develop essential communication skills and techniques.
www.learndirect.co.uk: government website with links to online courses.
www.bbc.co.uk/keyskills: online resources for practising communication skills.

| This brief has been verified as being fit for purpose | | | |
|---|---|---|---|
| **Assessor** | Simon Roberts | | |
| **Signature** | *Simon Roberts* | **Date** | *29 September 2010* |
| **Internal verifier** | John Talbot | | |
| **Signature** | *John Talbot* | **Date** | *29 September 2010* |

# Sample learner work

Conducting primary and secondary research could also be used to provide evidence towards Unit 3: Research Techniques for the Creative Media Industries.

## Task 1: Research plan + summary of information extracted (a)

### Initial ideas

Most teen interest magazines seem to have similar contents in terms of giving away free stuff and information on celebrities or events that are of interest to the audience.

I like the idea of looking at the specialist genre and working on a magazine that will celebrate graffiti and street art, allowing teens to get more information about and get involved in the scene.

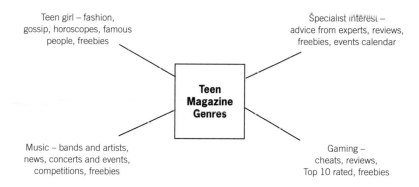

### Areas to research

Look at:
- designs and layouts of magazines to get a better idea of style and content
- similar magazines in a specialist (artistic) genre – how do they appeal to the audience and what do they include?
- creating a questionnaire to see if the idea appeals to a teen audience
- street art in the local area as well as nationally and see what could be included
- copyright issues and whether I would be able to publish work I can't track down the author of
- legality of graffiti and its popularity in today's culture.

### Primary research

*Questionnaire*

I had to conduct a questionnaire in order to get enough information on what people are interested in. I had to check if it is worthwhile to even start my production. It was a very important part of my research because it gave me an idea what I should focus on, how much do they know about the subject of my magazine, what would they want my magazine to include. I also had a chance to get to know some of the graffiti artists that I did not know before. Thanks to the questionnaire I had a possibility to narrow down my target audience. It helped me to cut out or put some more bits into my magazine. It gave me the idea if people are interested in graffiti-making and if they are doing it already how would they describe themselves (amateur, professional, etc.) which gave me an information on how I could make it suitable for all of those stages.

The learner has extracted a number of useful quotes from the research conducted which will go towards criterion 1 and inform the content of the magazine.

**Sample learner work: page 2**

*Questionnaire responses*
Here are the results of the questionnaire:

**Gender**
Female   13          Male      12

**Age**
10-13   3            14-16   6            17-19   10           20-25   4           20+   2

**Do you like graffiti?**
Yes     7            No      11          Some of them   7

**Do you think that graffiti is vandalism?**
Yes     5            No      5           Depends          15

**What do you think about designated places for graffiti ('legal walls')?**
Good    22           Bad     3           Don't Care       0

**Would you consider graffiti as a form of art?**
Yes     22           No      3           Some of them     0

**Do you know any graffiti artists?**
Yes     7            No      18

**Do you like to draw?**
Yes     11           No      5           Sometimes        9

**Have you ever tried to make graffiti (including on paper)?**
Yes     9            No      16

**If yes, at what stage do you think you are?**
Amateur  5           Advanced 4          Professional     0

**Would you like to learn how to create graffiti?**
Yes     11           No      14

**Would you buy a magazine about graffiti?**
Yes     7            Maybe   5           No       13

**If so what sort of things would you like to see in it.**
**Comments:**

"I'd like some good tutorials, theres nothing on the internet except using computers"
"It'd be kewl if it had interviews famous graffiti artists"
"I wanna know how to get involved in big graffiti projects"
"How not to get caught – lol"

This clearly shows the sources the learner has used to extract useful information for the report.

The learner has identified, with some precision, why the information is useful and has been included, which will go towards a merit in criterion 1.

**Sample learner work:** page 3

I looked on the internet and in magazines and found the following stuff that was useful to me for preparing my Treatment. I've copied and marked up the original articles which I can supply as an appendix to my research.

The following quote is from an article about the council pulling down a 'legal' graffiti wall in coventry.

"One local resident called the graffiti wall 'public art' and referred to it as 'better than much of the stuff you see in galleries.' Another said that the demolishing of the wall would be 'a loss to the local community.

When we talked to one of the artists who has been integral in developing many of the larger graffiti 'murals' he described how graffiti art differed from vandalism; 'the buildings were abandoned and we turned them into works of art. The sort of people who just spray tags in public places are vandals.'"

www.coventrychronicle.co.uk

One of the most famous graffiti artists is Banksy, though his work has also sometimes been described as vandalism as he creates it in very public places. However even Banksy's graffiti art has been subject to vandalism. It was reported that one of Banksy's murals in Park street, Bristol was 'defaced by vandals who splattered the image with blue paint sometime during the night.' (Bristoltoday.co.uk)

I contacted http://graffiti.org who have some great information on their website about why graffiti is popular. It says that in some communities there are classes teaching graffiti!

I also tried to find information on the target market for my magazine.

"Despite the emergence of the internet, magazine remain a popular media form, and many specialist magazines still thrive in niche markets"

www.Mediamagazines.com

"Teenage males offer largely untapped potential for publishers."

http://www.marketweek.co.uk

From these two quotes I believe that there is a market for my magazine.

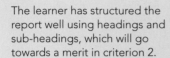

The learner has structured the report well using headings and sub-headings, which will go towards a merit in criterion 2.

The learner has shown how information on copyright extracted from a website is useful, which will go towards a merit in criterion 1.

**Sample learner work: page 4**

### *Similar products*

One part of my research was to look at similar products. I had to buy some magazines to see what features are significant for that type of magazine (teenager based, single interest, colourful, artistic, etc). It gives me also an idea on how much should I charge for it. Most of the magazines are around £4–5. Also the front covers gave me some inspiration on what teenagers and young adults are attracted to. The amount of pictures and text was also similar. Deeper research into similar products also assured me that there is no such product like mine so I think I found a gap in the market.

**Product research**

I came across the following specialist magazines:
Fused magazine
i-D
STEP Inside Design
JUXTAPOZ
spex

### *Internet*

I needed to find out if graffiti was covered by the laws of copyright and if it was if I would be able to reproduce it. There are many discussions and blogs about this on the internet, most of which centred on the legality of graffiti and whether or not it could be covered at all by copyright laws. The official UK Copyright website didn't really cover this but did say that copyright covered all artistic works including art, and graffiti, even illegal, is an art form.

The best solution I found was on the website listed below and I was able to conclude from this that I would be able to reproduce photographs of graffiti as long as I entered in the text below, which will help me get around this problem whilst covering me legally for displaying images of original artwork that isn't mine.

'Copyright owner of artwork unknown – uncommissioned artwork. Please advise if you are the copyright owner or know who they are.'

http://www.unimelb.edu.au/copyright/information/fastfind/artistic.html

### Secondary research

#### *Internet*
1 **Graffiti in Coventry**
   I needed to find some information on graffiti in my hometown in order to have some basic knowledge on where I stand. I needed to know where I could find graffiti, where some legal walls are and what are the legal restrictions in Coventry according to this type of art. I found some really nice locations and some graffiti artists which I will be able to use in my project.

Inset boxes help the presentation of the report and highlight particular information

**Sample learner work: page 5**

I was looking into places where graffiti could be found around our area and had seen these boards up around the rugby stadium, I wanted to know if these had been put up there for a purpose or if they had been 'vandalised'.

As you can see in my research below I discovered that they were legal, this is a real boost to the graffiti scene and an acknowledgement by the local council that this is a kind of art form, I have thought about covering this in the contents of the magazine and may follow this up by interviewing the people involved and highlighting the positive aspects of all this. I will see how well my pitch goes first and will then consider the detail of my contents a bit more, fine tuning my article ideas so to speak.

---

**Blog on local Graf website**

**Question**

Hey, can anyone tell me if the wooden boards covering the entire perimeter of the Rugby Stadium r legal? I guess they r only temporary??

**Response**

The boards are temporary because of the development at the old college next door. But the timescale is massive, they're not going any time soon. I was involved in securing the boards and artists have direct permission from the main man. Plenty of public attention.

---

2 **Well-known UK towns – Graffiti scene**
My first issue is going to be Coventry-based but I had to find some other towns for next issues. I found that Northampton had an illegal graffiti gallery, which was well known across the whole of Europe. It is also a good selling point that the UK has some well-known places. It could help if I wanted to expand my magazine to the other countries. It also proves that British graffiti culture is very strong so I will definitely find an interest in my product.

3 **Well-known UK artists – Graffiti scene**
One of the topics that my magazine will cover is graffiti artists. For my first issue I wanted someone who is British but known worldwide. I decided to go for artist called Banksy. He was mentioned a few times in the articles in some other countries. I found an article on him in the New York Times so it means they know him everywhere. It also proves (just like Northampton's illegal gallery) that the popularity of graffiti in Britain is still growing. This information helped in my pitch. It gave me a support to say that there is definitely an interest in graffiti in this country so I will sell my product without any problems.

**4   How to use InDesign software**

I am not that familiar with design software so I had to look for some help on the internet. I found some tutorials and lessons on how to use InDesign so it will save me time and money because in real life I would have to hire a designer and after these quick lessons I can do it myself.

**5   Magazines**

Apart from looking at similar products I had to research what the magazine should include, how it should look, how to lay out the content page and what I should I write on the cover to make it more eye catching. All of this information is very helpful and timesaving because if I did not find them on the internet I would have to conduct another questionnaire on how do you think magazines should look like and I would probably get too many answers which would just confuse me. I wanted to find (and I did) just a short and brief list of what I should include, what is necessary and what is not.

**Cover ingredients**

I consulted the following website: www.magforum.com/cover_secrets.htm. This looks at a front cover from Cosmopolitan magazine, and gives a chart to describe the ingredients of a front cover. The chart was very helpful as it showed me how to deconstruct a magazine front cover, highlighting what the relevant elements are that I will need to include in my magazine, even if it is going to be in a different genre I will need to consider what it is that the reader will expect to see, the codes and conventions if you like of magazine production.

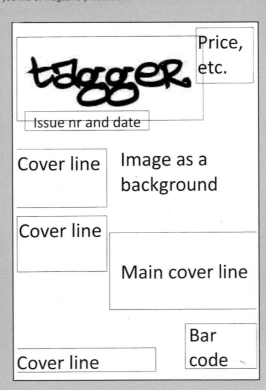

Useful annotations have been made and specific instances identified, this time in relation to grammar.

The learner has made useful annotations and identified specific instances where changes to spelling will lead to beneficial changes in the final report.

**Sample learner work: page 7**

## Task 2 : Proposal (evidence b–e)

### b) Draft proposal

#### Outline of production
I am going to make a print production. It is going to be a magazine cover, content page and article page. My magazine is going to be a graffiti fan magazine. I am going to include there some tutorials, tips etc. Mu idea is to create magazine which could be for professionals as well as for amateurs who would like to start to create urban art.

#### Purpose of production
The purpose of my production is to show that graffiti is not always vandalism. It can be a kind of art when made in designated area and it is not offending anyone. Another purpose is to encourage people to do something creative with their time. As I said I want it to be a magazine for everyone from beginners to advanced artists. And as it is a magazine the obvious purpose of it is to ear money. Shops (selling like sprays etc) can earn money on that project as well through advertising in my magazine.

#### Target audience
My target audience are mainly young people in age between 10–25 with some exceptions in both boundaries. But this I am going to focus on this age group. I believe that more boys are interested in graffiti making than boys so I have to make the magazine attractive especially for boys because boys will not like it pink where girls interested in urban art won't mind a magazine created with boys in mind.

So basically my typical consumer is boy/men in age of 10–25 interested in graffiti art, amateur or professional, probably in subculture connected to urban art.

#### Cast
I am going to need only few people to be models for tutorials of graffiti making and maybe in photos shoots in front of graffiti already existing. I am going to work with David because he is really interested in graffiti art style and he can make some simple but very attractive ones so it would be good for first issue as a starting point.

#### Meaning
My aim is to interest people in the form of art represented by graffiti and to show it in other way than horrible vandalism.

#### Locations
Most of my shots are going to be in closed space probably in David's room or my own. I will have to find a nice graffiti in town for the picture for the cover and for an illustration to article and others needs.

### c) Final proposal

#### Outline of production
I am going to make a print production. It is going to be a graffiti magazine with a contents page and article pages. My magazine is going to be a graffiti fan

*Needs to be more detailed. I need to include:*
- *Why I am doing this genre*
- *More on content*
- *Check spelling and grammar – I have to be more careful to pick up simple typing errors like "Mu idea" here and "to ear money" in the paragraph below*

*I need to bring this together more and check the content. I need to be more specific about what I want to put in it and what I want the audience to get from it.*

*I'm happy with my initial ideas on the target audience. I need to look in more detail at the results of my research and check I have my facts right here when it comes to my treatment. I really need to check the grammar too, I can see mistakes here when I say "people in age between" and "my typical consumer is boy/men in age of...".*

*These last three sections need bringing together and I need to include a lot more detail about each bit. I will need to make my ideas more obvious and try and sell them to the client.*

Here the annotations and suggestions relate to structure.

Most of the changes identified have been made to beneficial effect in the final proposal.

One of the changes identified in this paragraph was changed but the other was missed.

**Sample learner work:** page 8

magazine because I feel that there is a gap in the market for this type of product; my questionnaire results showed that a lot of people from different age groups will be interested in this type of thing. I am going to include some tutorials, tips etc. My idea is to create a magazine that could be for professionals as well as for amateurs who would like to start to create urban art.

### Purpose of production

The purpose of my production is to show that graffiti is not always vandalism. It can be a kind of art when made in designated areas and it is not offending anyone. I found out that it should be OK to print this art as long as I fully and clearly credit the artist that created it. Another purpose is to encourage people to do something creative with their time.

As I said I want it to be a magazine for everyone from beginners to advanced artists so another aim is to develop skills of those less familiar with the techniques. And as it is a magazine the obvious purpose of it is to earn money. Shops (selling like sprays etc) can earn money on that project as well through advertising in my magazine.

### Target audience

My target audience is mainly young people aged between 10–25 with some exceptions in both boundaries. But I am going to focus on this age group. I believe that more boys are interested in graffiti-making than girls so I have to make the magazine attractive for boys because boys will not like it pink whereas girls interested in urban art won't mind a magazine created with boys in mind. So basically my typical consumer is boys/men aged 10–25 interested in graffiti art, amateur or professional, probably in subculture connected to urban art.

### Other details
*Cast*

I am going to need only a few people to be models for tutorials of graffiti-making and maybe in photo shoots in front of already existing graffiti. I will use models that fit the culture and style of the magazine, making sure their dress is appropriate and will appeal to the target audience. I am going to work with David because he is really interested in graffiti art style and he can make some simple but very attractive ones for the tutorials, he is also involved in the scene and looks the part. I think it would be good for the first issue as a starting point.

*Meaning*

My aim is to interest people in the form of art represented by graffiti and to show it in other ways, not as horrible vandalism. I want to encourage a positive image and also encourage the readers to get involved in more legal forms of graffiti by providing details of organised events and locations nationwide. I really want to discourage the current negative stereotype associated with the scene.

*Locations*

Most of my shots are going to be in enclosed spaces probably in David's room or my own, this will be for the tutorial shots as I can control the lighting etc. I will have to find some nice graffiti in town for the pictures for the cover and for an illustration of articles, I will need to check for lighting conditions and find bold grafs that aren't too badly faded as I don't want to spend too much time Photoshopping the work, I also need to find ones relevant to my article so I need to spend quite a bit of time on recces.

New text has been added and a spelling mistake in this text was missed.

Useful annotations relating to clarity of expression are made here which will lead to beneficial changes in the final report.

The learner has made useful annotations and identified specific instances where changes to spelling and grammar will lead to beneficial changes in the final report.

**Sample learner work:** page 9

## d) <u>Draft treatment</u>

### Introduction

My fifth Idea is to create a magazine about graffiti. Its title would be 'Tagger'. It is going to be a tutorial- how to make graffiti as well (something similar to the 'how-to-draw-manga'-type thing). It would be printed out every fortnight.

My aim is to create something which would be suitable for people already common with the topic of graffiti and confident in making it as well for people who are beginners and amateurs in creating urban art. My other purpose of the magazine is to show that type of art in different light to which people are used to. I would like to convince people that graffiti is not always vandalism. Like I already mentioned it is going to be 'how-to...'-type of magazine which is very popular nowadays. There are some magazines on how to draw people, landscapes and other things but there are based o the idea of fine art not very popular among young people. The other one is 'Draw!' which is an American magazine on drawing cartoon characters.

As I am living in Coventry I decided to focus on graffiti placed in my area as they will be accessible. It might also work as a first issue so it could be said that in next one there will be works from different town. Because I chose my area to work in I had to conduct a research about graffiti in Coventry and neighbour towns to see where I can find them and what council and inhabitants thinks about urban art. My secondary research includes pictures of graffiti in Coventry area and some positive articles about them as well as negative ones. My primary research includes questionnaire about people thoughts of graffiti and I had to find someone who is familiar with this kind of art work to help me with tutorials and give me some instructions on what is interesting and what would be attractive to urban art fans.

### Distribution

My magazine would be on shelves every two weeks because I know on my own experience I do not like to wait whole month for a magazine which I like. Every week would be too frequent because it gives me too little time to complete complicated magazine which has to be very detailed in graphics as it is an artistic magazine. Most of the time spend would be on the visual aspect of it.

I would like it to be sold in every possible place just to attract as much people as it is possible because it is a new magazine so people need to get familiar with it and get used to it. I would sell it in all of the big supermarkets, newsagents, most of the smaller shop chains like 'Spar'.

I do not think there is huge competition because while I was doing my research I was looking for similar products but the only one I found was 'How to draw manga' and 'Draw!' which is being sell in US so both of them do not really have much to do with graffiti. Apart from that I was looking through some of the magazines for teens and young people and I found out that most of them were targeted to girls. The only magazines which were somehow aimed at boys were game magazines and as far as I know most of the subcultures have their own magazine and I think I found a gap in the market as there is no such product as mine.

*The entire style and layout of this needs to be improved as does the spelling and grammar, I have obviously speed typed this and made quite a few mistakes. MUST BE MORE FORMAL!!*

*I'm still making typing errors... This should read "but they are based on the idea"*

*It might be better if I say "from my own experience" or "in my own experience"*

*I need to be clearer about where and what format. Again quite a few errors, I am also starting to rethink the regularity, maybe I will look at monthly publications in more detail.*

The learner has made useful annotations and identified specific instances where changes to the structure of the report will lead to beneficial changes in the final report

### Target audience

My first thought about my target audience was that it is going to be a group of young people at age of 10–25. But after considering all of the characteristics of people in smaller groups like 10–15, 16–20 and 21–25 I decided to cut my main group to 15–25 because children under 15's might use graffiti in different way than I want to present it which would totally ruin my whole project. They are less responsible than over 15's so parents would not appreciate the idea of the magazine encouraging their children to the act of 'vandalism'. As the group of 15–25 is more mature there is a chance they will understand how to create this art without hurting anyone. So my typical customer would be a boy/man in age of 15–25 interested in the idea of graffiti whether amateur or already familiar with that style. There would be obviously some exceptions in the gender so I am counting on attracting some girls as well. As my magazine is going to be design with boys on mind I think that it would be interesting also for girls because if they are interested in urban art they might be a tomboy type or they will be just open-minded so they will not really pay attention to the design but to the content.

*This is also too cluttered and needs breaking down. Will also include results of my questionnaire to back this up.*

### Proposal

I am going to produce between 3 and 8 pages of graffiti magazine. This will include cover page, content page and some article pages. I would like to make one tutorial article and one article about graffiti itself or about graffiti artist.

The cover will have to include a title ('Tagger') which will have to be quite catchy and list of the main articles in the magazine to attract the potential customers. It will have to be quite colourful and it must include a picture of graffiti so the customer knows straight away what this magazine is about. I will have to take care of the obvious parts of the cover like issue number, date, and bar code as well. My target audience are young people (15–25) so I have to use fonts which would not be too boring but also not too childish. On my content page I will have to list all my articles and maybe write more about some of them just to interest the reader. On the content page I am going to include contact details and probably some adverts and maybe a contest. The next few pages would be based on articles. One of them will be a tutorial how to make graffiti. I want to start the magazine with the graffiti on paper not on the wall because my target audience include amateurs. I am going to ask my friend David Czerwniak to help me with this because I cannot draw graffiti myself. I will take close ups of him creating one and then I will write tips what to do. When I was doing my research I found out that many people do not know any of the graffiti artists so I decided I will go for Banksy for my first issue. I based my art essay on his work so I know he did not prohibit using his work. Most of the pictures in the magazine will be taken by me. The only exceptions will be pictures of Banksy's work. I might use some photos from Internet but only if I will not be able to take them myself. As I said the tutorial pictures will all be close ups so there will not be face shown, only hands and materials. For the photos of graffiti on walls I will have to look at the lighting and from what angle they will look the best so I cannot really decide what shot I will use. I might use tripod to increase the quality of the pictures.

*For the most part this is fine, again I need more detail, tidy it up and check spelling and grammar.*

> The learner has made useful annotations and identified specific instances where changes to the structure of the report will lead to beneficial changes in the final report.

**Sample learner work:** page 11

## Conclusion

In my opinion the biggest selling point is that the interest in area of graffiti is increasing with time. There are more and more people interested in this type of urban art. Also the contrast between different subcultures is getting bigger so the main characteristics of each group are getting more distinct. Every group is fighting for bigger audience and respect. I also think that this magazine should be made because there is nothing in the market like this product. I have done some research and I have found anything similar in the UK market. There was something about drawing in United States. So I am pretty confident that I have found a gap in the market at least in this country. But here comes also the weakness of my product. If there is not a product like mine, does it mean that there is no need for it? There is always a risk in new productions but according to my questionnaire it is worth it because most answers for 'Would you like to learn how to create graffiti?' were positive. Another weakness might be the copyright issue. I am not sure whether or not I am allowed to publish pictures of graffiti made by someone else but on the other side if they made it in public place it should probably be for public use as well so everyone should have right to it. Graffiti artists work anonymously so they do not revile their identity because graffiti is illegal in some places so they would not some out and say 'do not use it' because police could arrest them straight away. They are creating art to show something so they probably do not mind if they would be even more famous. When I was doing research I found some well-known website with graffiti from all over the world. I am pretty sure that graffiti artist did not submit their own work. As long as they were signed with the nick of the painter everything was all right. So I am not really concerned about the copyrights. The strengths of my magazine would be the facts that it is brand new and exciting for young people as finally someone got interested in their art. I might add the possibility of contacting other graffiti admirers and gallery of the readers work. I think that the idea of readers involved in creating magazine would be good as well. I could make a contest on the best article about graffiti and the winning articles would be printed in each issue. That would make my magazine more interactive so there would be a communication in both ways not only from magazine to readers but also from readers to magazine. That I think is very good selling point.

*This is a large block of text and really isn't user friendly. I need to make sure that all of my facts and opinions are substantiated and to check for any errors.*

*Oops, I meant 'reveal' here. I need to be careful not just to accept the first option the spell check gives me*

## e) <u>Final treatment</u>

### Introduction

The idea for this product is to create a magazine about graffiti, the title of which, research has shown, should be short and sweet in order to attract the target audience. The current working title I have come up with is Tagger as it fits the genre and culture of graffiti and 'tagging' which is what artists do in order to sign their work, therefore there is a sub-cultural connotation there.

The product is going to contain tutorials on how to make graffiti (something similar to the 'how-to-draw-manga'-type of magazine) and I ame hoping it will be a sort of graffiti 'fanzine' that will gain more attention from the TA through positive word of mouth. In order not to seem too patronising by seeming to try to tell graffiti artists how to draw we will also include more 'unifying' content, such details of legal events that taggers can go to in their local area.

> The learner has identified that proofreading is needed, not just electronic spellchecking.

**Sample learner work:** page 12

The product will be printed and distributed monthly. This decision is based on research, which has shown that other specialised magazines tend towards a monthly publication date in order to allow them time to source and create more content. It is important to bear in mind that there is only a certain amount of graffiti available and there are also limits on what can be shown due to legal and copyright issues as well as suitability of content.

My aim is to create something that would be suitable for people already familiar with the topic of graffiti and confident in making it, as well as for people who are beginners and amateurs in creating urban art. My other purpose for the magazine is to show this type of art in a different light from that which people are used to. I would like to convince people that graffiti is not always vandalism.

As I already mentioned it is going to be 'how-to' type of magazine, which is very popular nowadays. There are magazines on how to draw people, landscapes and other things, but they are commonly based on the idea of fine art, not very popular among young people. Although I did find one that might appeal to a younger audience, this one is called Draw!, which is an American magazine that focuses on drawing cartoon characters.

The main focus will be on graffiti placed in local areas throughout Britain. It will feature works from different artists in towns and cities, each month a new place, this will give readers something to look forward to as they look to see if it their town this time. I could also run competitions 'where should we go next?' readers could email their suggestions and the best one would have their artwork in the magazine and take us on a tour of the art in their town.

Primary research has been conducted including a questionnaire investigating people's thoughts on graffiti. The feedback so far has been extremely positive and as the target audience sections shows we have also had some positive responses from female participants. Copyright issues have also been looked into as there is the obvious problem of authorship, after all some tagging is done illegally and therefore the people doing it do not wish to advertise themselves. Findings seem to indicate that as long as a taggers' 'tag' is prominently displayed on the artwork and referenced in the write up or captions then they will be fully credited and copyright shouldn't be infringed.

**Distribution**

The product will be on the shelves of supermarkets and newsagents on a monthly basis. Weekly or fortnightly would be too frequent because it gives too little time to complete complicated magazine layouts, which have to be very detailed graphically. As it is an artistic magazine I have to be sure content is detailed and precise, most of the production time spent would be on the visual aspect of it.

There is also the potentiality to distribute this via a website or in some other e-media format. However, costs and income need to be considered and subscriptions would need to be set up before users could access information. While this is a viable idea for the modern market it would have to be considered at a later date, possibly once the magazine had been established, as there will be costs involved in setting this up and running it correctly. Also a print publication is more portable and taggers are often out and about doing their thing, so this may suit their needs better.

The learner has improved the structure of the proposal in line with the comments made when reviewing the draft document.

**Sample learner work: page 13**

It should be sold in every possible place nationwide in order to attract as many people as possible, it is a new magazine so people will need to get familiar with it and get used to it. There should be a campaign to launch it prior to distribution and this should be done on the internet via email and pop ups in chat rooms, etc. My research led me to conclude that this is where the target audience spend a lot of their time and are more likely to receive the information from here than from an expensive and complicated TV ad. Also, there aren't any similar products out there we could advertise in, although we should target specialist shops and websites that sell paint cans, etc. as this is where the target audience will shop.

In terms of generating sales, I do not think there is huge competition for my product because my research also shows that there is a lack of similar products. The only ones I found were How to draw Manga and Draw!, which are only sold in US (but can be bought in the UK via subscription) and neither of them really have much, if anything, to do with graffiti.

**Target audience**

My first thought about my target audience was that it is going to be a group of young people aged between 10–25. But after researching all of the characteristics of people in smaller groups like 10–15, 16–20 and 21–25 I decided to cut my main group to 15–25. This is because children under 15 might use graffiti in a different way than I want to present it (less responsibly), which would totally ruin the concept of the publication and how I want it to be viewed by the reader. This age group are less responsible than over 15s so parents would not appreciate the idea of the magazine encouraging their children to the act of what they might perceive as vandalism.

As the group of 15–25 is more mature there is a chance they will understand how to create this art without upsetting others or destroying property. So the typical customer would be a male aged 15–25 interested in the idea of graffiti, whether amateur or already familiar with that style. There would obviously be some exceptions so the product should also attract some girls as well, and the results of the questionnaire show that some females are interested in this type of product. The magazine is going to be designed specifically with boys in mind as they are the main creators of street art, however it would also appeal to some girls such as those interested in urban art, the tomboy type, simply artistic and open-minded so they will not really pay attention to the design but to the content.

When looking into the market and audience I targeted some of the magazines aimed at teens and young people and I found that most of them were targeted at girls, the only magazines which were somehow aimed at boys were either games magazines or music magazines (which tend to be more gender neutral) so again there is a gap in this particular market. I have also found that most of the teen 'subcultures' have their own magazine but not this one, the gap just keeps widening.

> The changes made to the final proposal have frequently had beneficial effect and will contribute towards a merit in criterion 3.

> The conclusions have been explained with clarity, which will contribute to a Merit in criterion 2.

**Sample learner work: page 14**

### Final proposal

The magazine is going to be between 30 and 40 pages long, A4 size with A3 pull out posters 'featured' in certain issues. The magazine will include a cover, which will be eye catching and feature the work of a prominent artist working in the featured town or city. It will also have a contents page so that people know where to look for articles featured on the front cover as well as the tutorial and other features sections. Much of the magazine will be dedicated to article pages and special features, but will also have readers' letters and comments pages as well as a layout dedicated to the artwork of readers who have written in to the magazine. Tutorial articles will be a regular feature and we will invite some of the famous names in graffiti to contribute to this with their own hot tips and comments.

The cover will have to include a title (Tagger), which will be quite catchy, as will the list of the main articles in the magazine to attract the potential customers. Through my research I found that people do not know many of the 'famous' graffiti artists. Banksy will feature in the first issue, with a profile of him and a breakdown of what he does and where, it will also include images of some of his work. The front page will have to be colourful and eye catching and it must include a picture of graffiti so the customer knows straight away what this magazine is about. It will also contain the obvious essential elements of a cover, such as issue number, date, and bar code.

My target audience is young people (15–25) so I will have to use fonts that would not be too boring but also not too childish. On the contents page I will list all the articles and maybe write more about some of them just to interest the reader. It will also include contact details and hopefully some adverts from national companies selling graffiti related products, such as spray paints, and a weekly contest to keep readers involved and wanting to buy the next copy to see if they have won.

The magazine's tutorials will start with the graffiti on paper not on the wall because the target audience include amateurs and this is how they will practise their artwork. For this I will take close-up pictures of an artist creating a design and then write tips on what to do. Most of the pictures in the magazine will be taken by a professional photographer; the only exceptions will be pictures of Banksy's work. For this I will need to use some photos from the internet but only if I am able to obtain relevant copyright clearance.

### Conclusion

In my opinion the biggest selling point is that interest in graffiti is increasing all the time; there are more and more people interested in this type of urban art and wanting to become involved in it. Also the contrast between different subcultures is getting bigger, so the main characteristics of each group are getting more distinct; every group is fighting for a bigger uptake and more respect. I also think that this magazine should be made because there is nothing in the market like this product, research has shown that there isn't anything similar in the UK market, there was something about drawing in United States but not in this genre so I am pretty confident that I have found a gap in the market, at least in this country.

But this might be the potential weakness of the product, if there is not a product like it, does it mean that there is no need for it? There is always a risk in new productions, however, according to my questionnaire this is not the case, and most answers for 'Would you like to learn how to create graffiti?' were positive and so I think the reaction to the product will be.

The strengths of this magazine would be the fact that it is brand new and exciting for young people; they will feel that someone finally got interested in their art. I think that the idea of readers being involved in creating and contributing to the magazine will be good as well. I must get the audience involved and engaged with the product, I could run a contest on the best article about graffiti and the winning articles would be printed in each issue. That would make the magazine more interactive so there would be communication in both directions not only from magazine to readers but also from readers to magazine; that has been proven to be a very good selling point. As previously discussed I could also eventually look into putting the magazine on the web and setting up blogs and chat rooms for readers to come to and discuss urban art, thus increasing the magazine's accessibility and visibility.

It's a good idea to keep notes expanding on each slide of a presentation rather than putting too much information on the slides themselves.

The first slides can be used to outline the topic of your presentation.

The learner has created an identity for the product on the opening slide which is used throughout the presentation to give a coherent feel.

**Sample learner work: page 16**

# Task 3: The pitch (evidence f–i)

*f) Notes for my pitch*

Ideas for a PowerPoint presentation.

**Slide 2 (The Idea):**
- Brand new
- Graffiti – art not vandalism
- Available for everyone

**Slide 3 (What is it?):**
- Tutorials easy to follow
- Articles – graffiti, artists
- Picture gallery
- Adverts – skate shops, shops with paints

**Slide 4 (Target audience):**
- Young, interested
- 15–25 year old
- Amateur and professionals
- Mainly boys – tomboy-girl – do not bother about colours and layout

**Slide 5 (Distribution):**
- Every 2 weeks
- Supermarkets, newsagents etc
- Make people used to it
- Only 3,500 copies of first issue – make it unique, collectable, even more interesting

**Slide 6 (Research):**
- Primary: questionnaire – most of the people are interested in learning how to create graffiti; little knowledge about artists
- Secondary research: websites, how popular, fast-growing

**Slide 7 (Gap in the market?):**
- Target audience
- UK cities known in Europe: Bristol and Northampton
- Still growing popularity
- No such magazine in the UK

**Slide 8 (Budget):**
- Budget around £9,050
- Includes: tutorial, crew, equipment, printing cost
- Magazine price around £4 (most magazines have similar price)
- 3,500 copies for £4.00 gives us £14,000
- Which gives us around £5,000 profit.
- Increase number of copies after first issue

1

2

3

Simple bullet point topics can engage the audience without telling them too much until you are ready to.

If you aren't confident you will need to make your script simple to follow. This learner has used it to help with stage directions too, like the reminder to smile.

More good stage directions to help try to engage the audience.

Simple graphics help to make the presentation interesting. You could also consider using charts, animations or even video clips.

**Sample learner work:** page 17

**Slide 9 (Copyright):**
- Public place – public work?
- Anonymously
- Own photos – right to the photo
- Permission if possible
- Name , town, place
- Banksy
- They want to have publicity

*g) Script*

1  **Welcome Ladies and Gentlemen...**
Introduce myself. Say who am I and what I am going to talk about. Hand out sheets and wait a while when they are reading it. Ask them nicely to pay attention to the PowerPoint.

2  **SMILE!** Check quickly the notes about 'The Idea' slide and say all of the points in the order given.
- Brand new
- Graffiti – art not vandalism
- Available for everyone

Wait a second then proceed to the next slide.

3  **Quick check of the notes and then read out loud the title of the slide on the screen. Again talk through the points:**
- Tutorials easy to follow
- Articles – graffiti, artists
- Picture gallery
- Adverts –skate shops, shops with paints

When saying something unique and new look at the people to make them believe you. Next slide.

4  **Check notes. Refer to the people who are listening to you. The target audience part is very important as this might appeal to them the most because they may have children. Look at the slide sometimes (not for too long) to make them interested in it.**
Points for target audience:
- Young, interested
- 15-25 year old
- Amateur and professionals
- Mainly boys – tomboy-girl – do not bother about colours and layout

5  **Check notes. Go quite quickly through time and places focus on why 3,500 copies.**
Point you should include:
- Every 2 weeks
- Supermarkets, newsagents etc
- Make people used to it

4

5

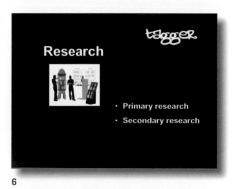

6

Once the basic idea is outlined in enough detail you need to expand on the information, adding information from criterion 4 content (Proposal), eg target audience, as the learner has done here.

The learner is using these later slides to expand on the content associated with criterion 4, in this case budget.

Be careful not to add too many stage directions or you might find them confusing.

**Sample learner work: page 18**

- Only 3,500 copies of first issue – make it unique, collectable, even more interesting

6  **Quick check of the notes as this is one of the easiest bits. Focus on the fact that you conducted primary research – quality! Say about:**
   - Primary: questionnaire – most of the people are interested in learning how to create graffiti; little knowledge about artists
   - Secondary research: websites, how popular, fast-growing

7  **The most important bit of the PowerPoint. Gap in the market. No place for hesitation. Confident. Need to speak slowly so they catch everything you are saying. They need to believe that this is the only occasion to make money on something original like your product. Points you need to make:**
   - Target audience
   - UK Cities known in Europe: Bristol and Northampton
   - Still growing popularity
   - No such magazine in the UK

   Remember to end with some catchy sentence and wait before next slide

8  **Budget. Check the notes because here are some numbers you need to remember. Mention that the amount of money needed for the production is not big in comparing to the profit it is going to bring. Say what budget includes. Price of the magazine needs to be mentioned. Points:**
   - Budget around £9,050
   - Includes: tutorial, crew, equipment, printing cost
   - Magazine price around £4.00 (most of magazines have similar price)
   - 3,500 copies for £4.00 gives us £14,000
   - Which gives us around £5,000 profit.
   - Increase number of copies after first issue

9  **You need to be very confident during this slide. This is quite difficult problem with making your magazine so you need to persuade them that you know everything about copyright in this matter. Keep eye contact – it will make you more believable. Start with the problems and end with the solutions. Points:**
   - Public place – public work?
   - Anonymously
   - Own photos – right to the photo
   - Permission if possible
   - Name, town, place
   - Banksy
   - They want to have publicity

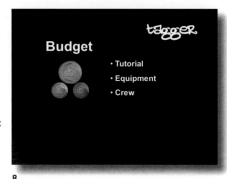

7

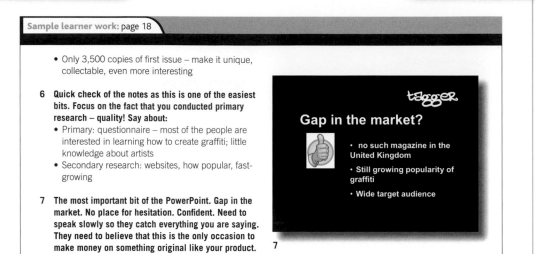

8

9

The learner is using these later slides to expand on the content associated with criterion 4, in this case copyright issues.

# Observation record

The observation report shows how the presentation could be improved, and highlights how this is linked to the two relevant criteria. It also shows the learner when they will have opportunities to improve these grades.

The tutor observed the presentation and the tutors comments on this can be used as evidence towards criteria 4 & 5. This is not instead of written learner evidence, but to support it. It's also a good idea to get presentations recorded as videos to be used as evidence, so you can play them back to watch your performance and identify where you can improve.

| Learner name | Mike Rogers |
|---|---|
| Qualification | BTEC Level 3 Creative Media Production |
| Unit number and title | Unit 2: Communication Skills for Creative Media Production |

**Description of activity undertaken (please be as specific as possible)**

Presenting pitch for teen magazine

**Assessment and grading criteria**

**P4** deploy and manage appropriate technology to pitch a media production proposal

**M4** deploy and manage technology to pitch a media production proposal effectively and with some imagination

**P5** employ appropriate forms of address in a media production pitch to communicate ideas

**M5** employ forms of address in a media production pitch to communicate ideas effectively

**How the activity meets the requirements of the assessment and grading criteria**

Your presentation was well prepared and you have put some effort into your PowerPoint slides, although the backgrounds were rather dark and could have benefited from being more vibrant to suit the style of your product.

You have made good use of clip art and imported pictures to illustrate your written work. however you could have had them move (the spray can, for example) or you could have added links to relevant sites (similar products such as *Drawing Manga*) so that the audience could have got a clear idea of the market.

You could improve this grade by adding more detail and creativity to your PowerPoint presentation, maybe some links to websites you looked at with relevant visuals or information. You could also improve the backgrounds for readability and add more targeted and slightly more detailed text.

You did prepare cue cards to help you during the presentation and your opening was very strong but then your performance started to tail off a little and you lost your place a couple of times, there wasn't any real flair to the overall content and layout and there were a couple of occasions when you got a little flustered and spoke too quietly; although you did your best to remain in role even when this happened. Probably a little more practice and a slower pace would have benefited you immensely. You will be given further opportunities to pitch proposals and you should bear this feedback in mind to try to improve on the merit grade you have been awarded for criteria 5.

All in all a good effort, well done Mike.

| Assessor signature | S. Roberts | Date | 7 February 2011 |
|---|---|---|---|
| Assessor name | Simon Roberts | | |

# Assessor's comments

| Qualification | BTEC Level 3 Creative Media Production | Year | 2010–2011 |
|---|---|---|---|
| Unit number and title | Unit 2: Communication Skills for Creative Media Production | Learner name | Mike Rogers |

| Grading criteria | Achieved? |
|---|---|
| **P1** use appropriate techniques to extract relevant information from written sources | Y |
| **P2** present a media production report which conveys relevant information | Y |
| **P3** review reports to make changes with occasional beneficial effects | Y |
| **P4** deploy and manage appropriate technology to pitch a media production proposal | Y |
| **P5** employ appropriate forms of address in a media production pitch to communicate ideas | Y |
| **M1** use appropriate techniques to extract information from written sources with some precision | Y |
| **M2** present a structured and detailed media production report which conveys information and explains conclusions with clarity | Y |
| **M3** review reports to make changes with frequent beneficial effects | Y |
| **M4** deploy and manage technology to pitch a media production proposal effectively and with some imagination | Y |
| **M5** employ forms of address in a media production pitch to communicate ideas effectively | Y |
| **D1** use appropriate techniques to extract comprehensive information from written sources | N |
| **D2** present a well-structured and substantial media production report which conveys information with precise exemplification and justifies conclusions with supporting arguments | N |
| **D3** review reports to make changes with consistently beneficial effects | N |
| **D4** deploy and manage technology to pitch a media production proposal with creativity and flair and to near-professional standards | N |
| **D5** employ forms of address in a media production pitch with flair to communicate ideas with impact | N |

**Learner feedback**

Overall I am happy with my grade but feel I could have worked harder on my presentation to give it have a better visual impact for the audience. I was very nervous presenting my ideas and that has obviously showed through, I think if I had practised and prepared more I could have done better and would like to try again at a later date if possible.

You should always read and take note of the assessor's feedback. Detailing what you enjoyed and also any problems that you had will help you in future assignments. It may also help your tutor when they come to revise the assignment, and this could help future learners.

### Assessor feedback

You have employed appropriate techniques to extract information from written sources and you have also managed to make contact with a primary source that proved both relevant and helpful. You have explained how the extracts are relevant to your proposal. I have seen your marked up and annotated originals but these need to be handed in as an accompanying appendix (**P1**, **M1**).

Your proposal and treatment are good working documents that are well structured and substantial (**P2**, **M2**). You have made changes by adding relevant information with beneficial effects (**P3**, **M3**), providing documents that convey information with precise exemplification and justify conclusions with supporting arguments (**M2**).

Your presentation was well planned and you had written up a script to help your through (**P4**, **M4**, **P5**, **M5**). However you could also have made use of handouts or even rough draft layouts of your product to provide the audience with some visual impact. You have made good use of clip art but there wasn't any real flair to the overall content and layout and there were a couple of occasions when you got a little flustered and spoke too quietly (see comments on observation sheet).

### Action plan

To achieve **D1**, you will need to seek out and research more written material on the subject. Provide printouts/copies with annotations to show how you have extracted information from the source and also provide a more detailed summary of why this written material is useful research for your propsal and treatment.

To achieve **D2**, you will need to provide more detail on the reasons for your choice of subject, justifying the production decisions you made, in response to your research findings. In particular, the statements you make in your conclusion need strong supporting arguments. For example, how sure are you that there are no other graffiti magazines available? Was your initial research comprehensive enough to make this statement?

To achieve **D3**, you will need to reveiw your proposal and treatment again to ensure that there are no further errors. Currently a few errors remain in your work.

To achieve **D4** and **D5**, you could add more detail and creativity to your PowerPoint presentation, maybe some links to websites you looked at with relevant visuals or information. You could also improve the backgrounds for readability and add more targeted and slightly more detailed text. In terms of your oral presentation you need to show more confidence and be more relaxed about presenting your information. You have some good, well researched ideas, let the audience see them in the best light and have confidence in them!

| Assessor signature | Simon Roberts | Date | 18 February 2011 |
| --- | --- | --- | --- |
| Learner signature | M. Rogers | Date | 20 February 2011 |

An action plan should list exactly what you need to do to improve your grade.

## Activity: Graffiti questionnaire

How would you answer the questionnaire given out in this assignment? Fill it in by circling your answers and filling in additional information where necessary.

**Gender**

Male        Female

**Age**

10–13        14–16        17–19        20–25        >25

**Do you like graffiti?**

Yes        No        Some of them

**Do you think that graffiti is vandalism?**

Yes        No        Depends

**What do you think about designated places for graffiti ('legal walls')?**

Good        Bad        Don't care

**Would you consider graffiti as a form of art?**

Yes        No        Some of them

**Do you know any graffiti artists?**

Yes        No

**If yes, which one/s?**

_____

_____

_____

**Do you like to draw?**

Yes        No        Sometimes

**Have you ever tried to make graffiti (including on paper)?**

Yes        No

**If yes, at what stage do you think you are?**

Amateur        Advanced        Professional

**Would you like to learn how to create graffiti?**

Yes        No

# Step Seven: Work productively as a member of a group

## Case study: Workplace teams

The web design team in a graphic design company in the north of England comprised a well-liked department manager who was nearing retirement, an account manager who liaised with the clients, a creative designer and a web developer. The team had always been regarded as successful until the department manager retired.

A new manager was appointed who had previously worked in the finance department. Within a month the team started missing deadlines and the account manager has complained to the company's directors that some clients have commented on the falling standard of the work.

The directors are very concerned about these falling standards and they have spoken to each member of the team. They have concluded that staff do not respect the new manager as he does not seem to value their skill sets or how they integrate as a team.

- The creative designer especially feels that the new manager is only interested in how quickly a job can be done, which doesn't help the creative process.

- Both the account manager and the creative designer feel that they should have been promoted, and so both have become very competitive, openly criticising both the new manager and each other.
- The web developer feels she had previously been a part of the whole process, as the previous manager had held regular team meetings where everyone could put forward ideas and give feedback. She thinks that the new manager just sees her as the end of a production line.

This short case study shows the importance of team cohesion and strong leadership, and how easily it can be lost. It is important that all team members share a common goal and have respect for each other.

### Reflection points

Think about other attributes that are essential for a successful team. What interpersonal skills do you think are needed to be a good team member? Do you think it is important for a team leader to have any additional interpersonal skills?

In your private life, you can choose your own friends, whereas at work you are paid to work alongside many people, whether you like them or not. This applies at school or college too. Hopefully, by now, you've outgrown wanting to only work with your best friends on every project.

You may not be keen on everyone in your team, but you should still be pleasant and co-operative. This may be harder if you are working with a partner than in a large group.

Sometimes you may be the group leader. This may inspire you, or fill you with dread. You won't be expected to develop team-leader skills overnight, but it helps if you know the basics.

First, you should understand how groups and teams work and why good teamwork is considered vital by employers.

# Working in groups and teams

If you have a full-time or part-time job, you already belong to a working group, or team. At school or college your class is an example of a working group.

All working groups have some common characteristics:

- doing the same type of work – though in the workplace you probably have different roles or responsibilities
- a group leader or supervisor
- a reason for working together, such as studying for the same qualification or tackling an area of work too large for someone to do alone
- group members are dependent on each other in some way; at work you may have to cover someone's workload if they are absent
- group members concentrate on their individual achievements and success.

A team is different. As a team member you have a specific objective to achieve **together** – and this is more important than the goals of individual team members.

## TOP TIP

Understanding how groups and teams function will help you be a better team worker and a better team leader.

These are the characteristics of a team.

- Team members have a team goal which is more important than any personal goals.
- Team members have complementary skills so that the team can achieve more than individuals working alone could achieve.
- Work is allocated to play to each person's strengths and talents.
- The team members give each other encouragement and support.
- There is collective responsibility for achieving the goal.

A good team leader acts as facilitator and motivator, and gives practical support and guidance.

Working in a team has many benefits. Team members can learn from each other and combine their skills to do a better job more quickly. Working with other people is often more enjoyable than working alone, too. Many industries rely heavily on efficient group working, from IT teams to health workers and the emergency services.

## TOP TIP

Focusing on the task rather than on personalities is the first step in learning to work with different people whose views may not match your own.

There are many benefits to be gained from working as a team.

# Being a good team member

Everyone wants team members who are talented, positive, cheerful and full of energy. These are the key areas to focus on if you wish to be a good team member.

- **Your social skills.** This includes being courteous, treating other people as you wish to be treated, saying 'please' when you want something and thanking people who do you a favour.

- **Your temperament.** Expect people to have different views and opinions from you, and don't take offence if someone disagrees with you. If you lose your temper easily, learn to walk away before you say something you may regret.

- **Your communication skills.** This includes talking and listening!

Practise saying what you mean clearly, accurately and succinctly. Be prepared to give good reasons to justify your arguments and ideas.

Allow people to finish what they're saying, without interruption, before you talk. Never shout people down. Think before you speak so that you don't upset people with tactless remarks. If you inadvertently do so, apologise.

- **Your commitment.** Always keep your promises and never let anyone down when they are depending upon you. Always do your fair share of the work, even if you don't agree with all the decisions made by your team. Tell people promptly if you are having problems so there is time to solve them. Be loyal to your team when you're talking to other people.

# Being the team leader

It can be difficult to strike a balance between 'leading' the team and working with friends. You need to inspire and motivate your team without being bossy or critical.

## Important points to remember about being a team leader

- Lead by example. Stay pleasant, consistent and control your temper, even under pressure.

- Everyone is different. Your ways of working may not always be the best.

- Be prepared to listen and contribute positively to a discussion.

- Encourage quieter team members to join in discussions by asking for their views.

- Be prepared to do whatever you ask other people to do.

- Note down what you say you will do, so that you don't forget.

- Discuss alternatives with people rather than giving orders.

- Be sensitive to other people's feelings. They may have personal problems or issues that affect their behaviour.

- Learn the art of persuasion.

- Act as peacemaker. Help people reach a compromise when necessary.

- Give team members the credit for their hard work or good ideas.

- Admit your mistakes. Look for a positive solution and think about what can be learned for the future, rather than making excuses.

- Praise and encourage team members who are working hard.

- Make criticisms constructively, and in private.

- Be assertive (put forward your point of view firmly) rather than aggressive (attacking other people to defend yourself).

## Some notes of caution about being a team leader

- Try to look pleasant and don't glare at people who interrupt you unexpectedly.

- Never talk about team members behind their backs.

- Don't gossip, exaggerate to make a point, spread rumours, speculate or tell lies.

- Don't expect to get your own way all the time – all good leaders back down on occasion.

- Never criticise any colleagues in front of other people. Speak to them in private and keep it constructive.

### TOP TIP

Excellent ideas often come from quiet team members. Encourage everyone to make suggestions so that you don't overlook any valuable contributions.

## Key points

- There are many benefits of working in a group or as a team. These include mutual support, companionship and the exchange of ideas.
- You will be expected to work co-operatively with other people at work, and during many course assignments.
- It isn't easy learning to be a team leader. Team leaders should be fair, consistent and pleasant to work with, as well as loyal and sensitive to the needs of team members.

## Action points

1 Identify the role of teamwork in your area of study. Identify the team's goal and any factors you think will contribute towards its success.

2 Decide how you would handle each of the following difficult situations if you were the team leader. If you can, discuss your ideas with a friend in your class.
   a) The team needs to borrow a college video camera to record an event being held tonight. Your tutor tells you that the one you reserved last week is not working and the rest are out on loan.
   b) A member of your team has personal problems so you have given him less work to do. Now you've been accused of having favourites.
   c) A team member is constantly letting everyone down because of poor work and non-attendance at group meetings.
   d) Two team members have disagreed about how to do a task. You're not bothered how they do it as long as it gets done properly, and by the deadline.
   e) A team member becomes very aggressive whenever she is challenged in any way – no matter how mildly.

3 Identify someone who has inspired you because they've been an excellent leader. This could be someone you've met, a fictional character or a famous person. Note down what it is about them that impressed you.

### TOP TIP

Team working, and bouncing ideas around, produce quicker and better results than working in isolation. Creative industries actively encourage team working.

## Activity: Valuing individual team members

Suppose you are chairing a meeting to discuss ideas for a production. Think about how you might handle these two situations.

• Raoul has nearly finished presenting his ideas when Sam interrupts him: 'Your ideas are stupid. I'll bet everyone here thinks the same, so let's just move on to the next person.'

• During the discussion, you notice that Daniel, who always tends to be reticent, hasn't said anything. No one else seems to have noticed, or to really care, whether every member of the team has had a chance to express an opinion.

Do you think it is important that everyone in the team has a say in group decisions? Ask other learners what they think they would do in these situations. Do you agree with them?

# Step Eight: Understand how to research and analyse information

## Case study: Finding and analysing information about jobs

When studying for a BTEC Level 3 National in Creative Media Production, you may be asked to carry out research for several reasons. For example, you might be asked to research:

- the history of the technology used in a particular media sector, such as animation or the print industry
- the roles and responsibilities associated with particular job roles in the media.

You may also be asked to research material that may not relate directly to the media industry but which could be information to be used to inform the content of a piece of work. For example, if you are designing an anti-smoking campaign website you may need to conduct research to find out the percentage of young people who smoke and the reasons why they start. This will help you produce a more effective website.

Some of the research you will undertake will be done individually. However, many projects will involve carrying out research in small groups and sharing the results with the whole team.

As part of Unit 3. Research Techniques for the Creative Media Industries, a group of four learners have been asked to conduct research into which new movies are most popular with young people.

They meet to come up with ideas for the type of research they should undertake, and come up with this list of suggestions:

- search the internet for statistics
- review current film magazines
- go on to movie chatrooms, forums and movie review sites
- go to cinemas and talk to the managers and staff
- draw up a questionnaire to give to young people to find out which films they have recently watched and enjoyed.

These learners are very sensible to consider several different methods of research. Even though plenty of information can be found on the internet, what problems do you think there might be restricting the research to material found on the internet?

### Reflection points

What problems do you think there might be if your only research was to question a group of your friends?

Think about the various methods that the learners in this case study propose to use. What might be the best ways to present the information they intend to collect?

As a BTEC Level 3 National learner, you often have to find information for yourself. This skill will be invaluable in your working life, and if you continue your studies at higher education level. Sometimes the information will give you a better understanding of a topic, at other times you will research information for a project or assignment. Sometimes you may be so interested in something that you want to find out more without being told to do so!

Whatever your reason, and no matter where your information can be found, there is a good and not so good way to go about the task. This section will help if you can't find what you want, or find too much, or drift aimlessly around a library, or watch a demonstration and don't know what to ask afterwards.

# Types of information

There are many types of information and many different sources. Depending on the task, these are the sources you may need to consult.

- **Verbal information.** This includes talking to friends, colleagues at work, members of your family, listening to experts explain what they do, interviewing people, talking to sales reps at an exhibition or customers about a product.

- **Printed information.** This includes information printed in newspapers, journals, magazines, books, posters, workshop manuals, leaflets and catalogues. The type of magazine or newspaper you read may have its own slant on the information, which you may have to take into account (see page 77).

- **Written information.** This includes course notes and handouts, reports and other documents in the workplace. If you want to use written information from work, you must check this is allowed, and that it doesn't contain confidential material such as financial information or staff names and addresses.

- **Graphical information.** This includes illustrations, pictures, cartoons, line drawings, graphs and photographs. Graphics can make something clearer than words alone. For example, a satnav instruction book might contain illustrations to show different procedures.

- **Electronic information.** This includes information from electronic sources such as DVDs, CD-ROMs, searchable databases, websites, podcasts, webinars (**seminars** online), emails and text messages. The huge amount of information available online is both a help and a hindrance. You can find information quickly, but the source may be unreliable, out of date, inaccurate or inappropriate (see page 76.)

## TOP TIP

Too much information is as bad as too little, because it's overwhelming. The trick is to find good-quality, relevant information and know when to call a halt to your search.

## TOP TIP

Consider all appropriate sources and don't just rely on information found online.

## Finding what you need

Spend a few minutes planning what to do before you start looking for information. This can save a lot of time later on.

The following steps will help you to do this.

1 Make sure you understand exactly what it is you need to know so that you don't waste time looking for the wrong thing.

2 Clarify your objectives to narrow down your search. Think about why the information is wanted and how much detail you need. For example, learners studying BTEC Nationals in Engineering and Performing Arts may both be researching 'noise' for their projects, but they are likely to need different types of information and use it in different ways.

3 Identify your sources and check you know how to use them. You need to choose sources that are most likely to provide information relevant to your objectives. For example, an engineering learner might find information on noise emissions in industry journals and by checking out specialist websites.

4 Plan and schedule your research. Theoretically, you could research information forever. Knowing when to call a halt takes skill. Write a schedule that states when you must stop looking and start sorting the information.

5 Store your information safely in a labelled folder. This folder should include printouts or photocopies of articles, notes about events you have attended or observed, photographs you've taken or sketches you've drawn. Divide your information under topic headings to make it easier to find. When you're ready to start work, re-read your assignment brief and select the items that are most closely related to the task you are doing.

# Primary and secondary research, and the law of copyright

There are two ways to research information. One is known as primary research, the other is secondary research.

## Primary research

Primary research involves finding new information about an issue or topic. This might include finding out people's views about a product or interviewing an expert. When carrying out interviews, you will need to design a survey or questionnaire. Your primary research might also include observing or experiencing something for yourself, and recording your feelings and observations.

## Secondary research

Secondary research involves accessing information that already exists in books, files, newspapers or on CD-ROMs, computer databases or the internet, and assessing it against your objectives.

This information has been prepared by other people and is available to anyone. You can quote from an original work provided you acknowledge the source of your information. You should put this acknowledgement in your text or in the bibliography to your text; do not claim it as your own research. You must include the author's name, year of publication, the title and publisher, or the web address if it is an online article. You should practise listing the sources of articles so

that you feel confident writing a bibliography. Use the guidance sheet issued by your centre to help you. This will illustrate the style your centre recommends.

The trick with research is to choose the best technique to achieve your objectives, and this may mean using a mix of methods and resources. For example, if you have to comment on an industry event you might go to it, make notes, interview people attending, observe the event (perhaps take a video camera), and read any newspaper reports or online comments.

# People as a source of information

If you want to get the most out of interviewing someone, or several people, you need to prepare carefully in advance.

The following points give some general advice about getting the most out of face-to-face interviews.

- Make sure you know what questions to ask to get the information you need.
- Explain why you want the information.
- Don't expect to be told confidential or sensitive information.
- Write clear notes so that you remember who told you what, and when. (See also page 78.)
- Note the contact details of the person you are interviewing and ask whether they mind if you contact them again should you think of anything later or need to clarify your notes.
- Thank them for their help.

If you want to ask a lot of people for their opinion, you may want to conduct a survey. You will need to design a questionnaire and analyse the results. This will be easier if you ask for **quantitative** responses – for example yes/no, true/false or ratings on a five-point scale – rather than opinions.

- Give careful thought to your representative sample (people whose opinions are relevant to the topic).
- Decide how many people to survey so that the results mean something.
- Keep the survey relatively short.

- Thank people who complete it.
- Analyse the results, and write up your conclusions promptly.

## TOP TIP

Test your questionnaire on volunteers before you 'go live' to check that there are no mistakes and the questions are easy to understand. Make any amendments before you conduct your 'real' survey.

Asking someone who knows a lot about a topic can be informative.

## Avoiding pitfalls

Wikipedia is a good online source that covers many topics, and often in some depth. It is popular and free. However, it has an open-content policy, which means that anyone can contribute to and edit entries. People may post information, whether it is correct or not. Wikipedia is moving towards greater checks on entries, but it is still sensible to check out information you find on this site somewhere else.

Apart from inaccuracy, you may find other problems with information you obtain through research, especially material found online.

- **Out-of-date material.** Check the date of everything and keep only the latest version of books, newspapers or magazines. Yesterday's news may be of little use if you are researching something topical.

- **Irrelevant details.** Often, only part of an article will be relevant to your search. For example, if you are forecasting future trends in an area of work, you do not need information about its history or related problems. When learners are struggling, they sometimes 'pad out' answers with irrelevant information. If you've researched properly you can avoid this by having enough relevant information for your purposes.

- **Invalid assumptions.** This means someone has jumped to the wrong conclusion and made 2 + 2 = 5. You might do this if you see two friends chatting and think they are talking about you – whether they are or not! You can avoid problems in this area by double-checking your ideas and getting evidence to support them.

- **Bias.** This is when people hold strong views about a topic, or let their emotions or prejudices affect their judgement. An obvious example is asking a keen football fan for an objective evaluation of their team's performance!

- **Vested interests.** People may argue in a certain way because it's in their own interests to do so. For example, when the government said Home Information Packs must be prepared for all properties being sold, the Association of Home Information Pack Providers was in favour because it trains the people who prepare the packs. The National Association of Estate Agents and Royal Institution of Chartered Surveyors were not because they thought they would lose business if people were put off selling their houses.

> **TOP TIP**
>
> Don't discard information that is affected by bias or vested interests. Just make it clear you know about the problem and have taken it into account.

## Reading for a purpose

You may enjoy reading or you may find it tedious or difficult. If so, it helps to know that there are different ways to read, depending on what you're doing. For example, you wouldn't look for a programme in a TV guide in the same way that you would check an assignment for mistakes. You can save time and find information more easily if you use the best method of reading to suit your purpose. The following are some examples of ways of reading.

- **Skim reading** is used to check new information and get a general overview.
To skim a book chapter read the first and last paragraphs, the headings, subheadings and illustrations. It also helps to read the first sentence of each paragraph.

> **TOP TIP**
>
> News articles are written with the key points at the beginning, so concentrate on the first paragraph or two. Feature articles have a general introduction, and important information is contained in the main text.

- **Scanning** is used to see whether an article contains something you need – such as key words, dates or technical terms.
Focus on capital or initial letters for a name, and figures for a date. Technical terms may be in bold or italics.

- **Light reading** is usually done for pleasure when you are relaxed – for example, reading a magazine article. You may not remember many facts afterwards, so this sort of reading isn't suitable for learning something or assessing its value.

- **Word-by-word reading (proofreading)** is important so that you don't miss anything, such as the dosage instructions for a strong medicine. You should proofread assignments before you submit them.

- **Reading for study (active reading)** means being actively involved so that you understand the information. It is rare to be naturally good at this, so you might have to work to develop this skill.

## Developing critical and analytical skills

Developing critical and analytical skills involves looking at information for any flaws in the arguments. These skills are important when you progress to work or higher education (HE), so it's useful to practise them now on your BTEC Level 3 National course.

A useful technique for understanding, analysing, evaluating and remembering what you are reading is **SQ4R**.

SQ4R is an effective method. It consists of six steps.

**1 Survey** first, to get a general impression. Scan the information to see what it is about, when it was written and by whom. The source, and the reason it was written, may be important. Most newspapers, for example, have their own 'slant' that affects how information is presented.

**2 Question** your aims for reading this material. What are you hoping to find? What questions are you expecting it to answer?

**3 Read** the information three or four times. The first time, aim to get a general idea of the content. Use a dictionary to look up any new words. Then read more carefully to really understand what the writer means.

**4 Respond** by thinking critically about the information and how it relates to the topic you are studying. Does it answer your queries partially, fully or not at all? What information is factual and what is based on opinion? Is there evidence to support these opinions? Is there a reason why the author has taken this standpoint? Do you agree with it? How does it link to other information you have read? What is the opposite argument and is there any evidence to support this? Overall, how useful is this information?

**5 Record** the information by noting the key points. Use this to refresh your memory, if necessary, rather than re-reading the article.

**6 Review** your notes against the original to check you have included all important points. If you are also preparing a presentation, reviewing your notes will help you to remember key points more easily.

## TOP TIP

SQ4R is just one method of reading for study. Research others and adapt them to suit your own style.

## Taking good notes

There are many occasions when you need to take notes, such as when a visiting speaker is talking to your class. There's no point taking notes unless you write them in a way that will allow you to use them later.

Note-taking is a personal activity. Some people prefer to make diagrammatical sketches with key points in boxes linked by arrows, others prefer to write a series of bullet points. You will develop your own style, but the following hints and tips might help you at the start.

- Use A4 lined paper, rather than a notebook, so that you have more space and don't need to turn over so often.
- When you're reading for study, make sure you have a dictionary, pen, notepad and highlighter to hand.
- Leave a wide margin to record your own comments or queries.
- Put a heading at the top, such as the speaker's name and topic, as well as the date.
- If you are making notes from a book or an article, remember SQ4R and read it several times first. Your notes will only be effective if you understand the information.
- Don't write in complete sentences – it takes too long.
- Leave spaces for later additions or corrections.
- Use headings to keep your notes clear and well organised.
- Only write down relevant information, including key words and phrases.

- Highlight, underline or use capitals for essential points.
- Never copy chunks of text – always use your own words.
- Clearly identify quotations and record your sources, so that you can cite them in your work. (Note the author's name, title, publisher, date and place of publication and the page number.)

## TOP TIP

Make sure your information is accurate, up to date, relevant and valid. Be aware of bias, and don't confuse fact with opinion.

## Key points

- Useful information may be verbal, printed, written, graphical or electronic.
- Effective research means knowing exactly what you are trying to find and where to look. Know how reference media are stored in your library and how to search online. Store important information carefully.
- Primary research is original data you obtain yourself. Secondary research is information prepared by someone else. If you use this, you must quote your sources in a bibliography.
- You can search for information by skimming and scanning, and reading in different ways. Reading for study means actively involving yourself with the text, questioning what you are reading and making notes to help your own understanding.
- Read widely around a topic to get different viewpoints. Don't accept everything you read as correct. Think about how it fits with other information you have obtained.
- Taking notes is a personal skill that takes time to develop. Start by using A4 lined pages with a margin, set out your notes clearly and label them. Only record essential information.

## Action points

- Working with a friend, look back at the sources of information listed on page 74. For each type, identify examples of information relevant to your course that you could obtain from each source. See how many you can list under each type.
- Check your ability to find the information you need by answering each of the questions in **Activity: Finding information** on the next page. For any questions you get wrong, your first research task is to find out the correct answers as quickly as you can.
- Go to page 108 to find out how to access a website where you can check your ability to skim and scan information, improve your ability to differentiate fact from opinion, summarise text and much more.
- Check your ability to sort fact from opinion and spot vested interests by completing **Activity: Let's give you a tip...** on page 82. Check your ideas with the answers on page 107.

## TOP TIP

Make a note of any information that you are struggling to understand so that you can discuss it with your tutor.

## Activity: Finding information

Answer the following questions about finding information.

**a)** Four types of information that are available from the library in your centre, besides books, are:

1

2

3

4

**b)** When I visit the library, the way to check if a book I want is available is:

**c)** The difference between borrowing a book on short-term loan and on long-term loan is:

Short-term loan:

Long-term loan:

**d)** The journals that are stocked by the library that are relevant to my course include:

**e)** Useful information on the intranet at my centre includes:

**f)** Searchable databases and online magazines I can access include:

**g)** The quickest way to check if a book or journal contains the type of information I need is to:

**h)** The difference between a search engine, a portal, a directory site and a forum is:

**i)** Bookmarking useful websites means:

**j)** In addition to suggesting websites, Google can also provide the following types of information:

**k)** Specialist websites which provide useful information related to my course include:

**l)** Useful tips I would give to people starting on my course who need to find out information are:

## Activity: Let's give you a tip...

In 2009, many businesses were struggling thanks to the credit crunch and falling consumer demand. Some, like Woolworths, closed down altogether. Others laid off staff, or announced wage cuts. Despite this, the government approved recommendations by the Low Pay Commission to increase the minimum wage rate from October. Although the rise was only small, many unions, including Unison and Usdaw, agreed it was better than a freeze, which had been wanted by the British Chambers of Commerce and the British Retail Consortium.

The government also announced new laws to stop restaurants and bars using tips to top up staff pay to the minimum level. *The Independent* newspaper claimed its 'fair tips, fair pay' campaign had won the day. It also reported that the British Hospitality Association was claiming this could result in up to 45,000 job losses. The Unite union also carried out a campaign and its General Secretary claimed the decision a triumph for the poorly paid. Not everyone agreed. Some thought there should be no tipping at all, as in Australia. Others said the Canadian system was best – wages are low but generous tips are left, and this motivates staff to give excellent service.

**a)** Look at the table below. In your view, which of the statements are facts and which are opinions? In each case, justify your view.

| Statement | Fact or opinion? | Justification |
|---|---|---|
| **i)** Having a national minimum wage helps low-paid workers. | | |
| **ii)** Over one million people will benefit from the minimum wage increase. | | |
| **iii)** The new law on tips will stop restaurants paying below minimum wage rates. | | |
| **iv)** Using the Australian system of no tips would be better. | | |
| **v)** The Canadian system guarantees good service. | | |
| **vi)** 45,000 job losses will occur in the hospitality industry. | | |

**b)** All newspapers have their own way of putting forward the news. Go to page 108 to find out how you can access a website which will help you to compare the way that news is reported in different newspapers.

Compare six different newspapers and make notes on:
**i)** the type of stories covered

_____

_____

_____

_____

_____

_____

_____

**ii)** the way views are put forward.

_____

_____

_____

_____

_____

_____

_____

_____

## Activity: How to go about your research

Saleem has devised a short questionnaire to find out what games and platforms are currently popular with 30–45-year-olds.

He has included the following questions:

- Q1: Do you agree the Nintendo DS is by far the most popular platform for 30–45-year-olds? YES/ NO
- Q2: What games do you think 30–45-year-olds would like and why?
- Q3: If you are 30–45 years old, would you like playing brain training and arcade games? YES/NO

Saleem intends to give the questionnaire to the other learners in his class to complete.

Do you think there is anything wrong with Saleem's strategy? Give reasons for your answer.

What changes would you suggest that Saleem should make to improve his research?

# Step Nine: Make an effective presentation

## Case study: Well-prepared presentations

Emma has recently secured her first job as a creative in the advertising industry and she has just made her first pitch, presenting her ideas for a corporate video to a group of clients.

She had given presentations during her National Diploma in Creative Media Production at college but she was still very nervous beforehand. She was particularly worried that the clients might not like her ideas, and felt that this would reflect badly on her. She took comfort from the advice of her tutors that if someone criticises your ideas it doesn't mean that they are criticising you, so you shouldn't take it personally.

She prepared by creating a PowerPoint presentation and making some fuller notes for herself, including some answers to questions she thought she might be asked. She rehearsed the presentation several times in front of a mirror in the days leading up to the client meeting. She also produced some handouts of her ideas (laid out in full colour) for the clients to take away.

So how did it go? 'Well, I'm really glad to have got that over with, but really, worrying about it beforehand was the hardest part.

'The clients were really friendly. I chatted with them and my boss over a coffee before the presentation. I think they realised I was a little nervous but they didn't seem to mind.

'I presented three ideas to them. They didn't say much when I presented the first idea, so I got the feeling they didn't like it much, but I didn't mind as I'd left the idea I liked best until last. During the second idea they started asking a lot of questions and were quite enthusiastic about how it might work. They seemed to quite like the third idea too, which was my favourite, but when I'd finished they asked to see the second idea again. They suggested a couple of small changes, but said this was the one they wanted to work with.

'I was really pleased they liked any of my ideas, but my boss said he'd had confidence in me all along.'

### Reflection points

Do you get nervous when you have to give a presentation for a college assignment? How do you prepare beforehand? Is there anything else that you could do to help you to feel more confident?

Making a presentation can be nerve-wracking. It involves several skills, including planning, preparation and communication. It tests your ability to work in a team, speak in public and use IT (normally PowerPoint). You also have to stay calm under pressure. However, as it is excellent practice for your future, you can expect presentations to be a common method of assessing your performance.

## TOP TIP

When you're giving a presentation, keep to time and get to the point quickly so that you use your time well.

## Good planning and preparation

Being well prepared, and rehearsing beforehand, help your confidence and your presentation. The following points will help you to do this.

- If you're part of a team, find out everyone's strengths and weaknesses, and divide work fairly taking these into account. Decide how long each person should speak, who should introduce the team, and who will summarise at the end.

- Take into account the time you have been allocated, your resources and team skills. A simple, clear presentation is better – and safer – than a complicated one.

- If you're using PowerPoint, make slides more interesting by avoiding a series of bulleted lists and including artwork. Print PowerPoint notes for the audience. Use a fuller set of notes for yourself, as a prompt.

- Check the venue and time.

- Decide what to wear and check it's clean and presentable.

- Prepare, check and print your handouts.

- Decide, as a team, the order in which people will speak, bearing in mind the topic.

- Discuss possible questions and how to answer them.

- Rehearse beforehand to check your timings.

If you prepare properly, you can really enjoy giving a presentation.

### TOP TIP

Rehearsing properly allows you to speak fluently, just glancing at your notes to remind you of the next key point.

On the day, you can achieve a better performance if you:

- arrive in plenty of time
- calm your nerves by taking deep breaths before going in front of your audience
- introduce yourself clearly, and smile at the audience
- avoid reading from your screen or your notes
- explain what you are going to do – especially if giving a demonstration – do it, and then review what you've done
- say you will deal with questions at the end of any demonstration
- answer questions honestly – don't exaggerate, guess or waffle
- respond positively to all feedback, which should be used to improve your performance next time.

## TOP TIPS

Make sure you can be heard clearly by lifting your head and speaking a little more slowly and loudly than normal.

## Key points

- When making a presentation, prepare well, don't be too ambitious, and have several rehearsals.
- When giving a demonstration, explain first what you are going to do and that you will answer questions at the end.

## Case study: Learner quotes about making presentations

Most people start off feeling uncomfortable about talking in front of a group of people, whether you know them or not. This is what some real learners have said about having to give presentations as part of their BTEC course.

'I used to dread presentations on my course, but found that if I went through my notes again and again until I knew the presentation inside out, it made it much easier and the presentations generally went well.'

**Javinder, 17, BTEC Level 3 National in Construction**

'I used to hate presenting to other people on my course, until I realised that most of them were as nervous about it as I was!'

**Koichi, 21, BTEC Level 3 National in Art and Design**

'Less is more! I used to rely on props, and as I was nervous about forgetting things or running out of things to say, I talked far too quickly. I had to repeat everything as nobody knew what I was on about! Some of my best presentations have been done without using slides or any other props at all, just talking (slowly of course) to my audience.'

**Laura, 18, BTEC Level 3 National in Health & Social Care**

'I used to be petrified of talking in front of other people but over time I've learned that, if I prepare well before a presentation, I usually feel much more confident on the day. If I know my material, I don't have to look down at my notes all the time and can make eye contact with the audience. Taking a few deep breaths before I begin keeps me calm and allows me to focus.'

**Katie, 19, BTEC Level 3 National in Creative Media Production**

'I prefer to be assessed by oral presentations as I'm dyslexic and my written work lets me down all the time. Everyone tells me that I really shine and show that I know my stuff when I present it to the rest of the group.'

**Sam, 17, BTEC Level 3 National in Business**

## Activity: All right on the night?

Read the following account and answer the questions that follow.
If possible, compare ideas with a friend in your class.

Gemma looked around in exasperation. The team were on the final rehearsal of their presentation and nothing was going right. Amaya seemed to think it was funny. 'Honestly, Gemma, why don't you just chill for a bit?' she suggested. 'You know what they say – a bad dress rehearsal means we'll do really well tomorrow!'

Gemma glared at her. 'Well, can I make a suggestion, too, Amaya,' she retorted. 'Why don't you just concentrate for a change? Sprawling around and dissolving into giggles every five minutes isn't helping either.'

She turned to Adam. 'And I thought you were going to build a simple model,' she said, 'not one that falls apart every time you touch it.'

Adam looked crest fallen. 'But I wanted to show how it worked.'

'How it's supposed to work, you mean!' raged Gemma, all her worries and anxieties now coming to the fore. 'We'll look stupid if it ends up in bits on the floor tomorrow and Amaya just falls about laughing again.'

'And Imran,' continued Gemma, turning her sights on the last member of the team, 'why is it so difficult for you to count to three minutes? We've agreed over and over again we'll each talk for three minutes and every time you get carried away with the sound of your own voice and talk for twice as long. It just means we're going to overrun and get penalised. And stop trying to wriggle out of answering questions properly. For heaven's sake, if you don't know the answer, how hard is it just to say so?'

Silence fell. No one looked at each other. Adam fiddled with his model and something else fell off. Amaya wanted to laugh but didn't dare.

Imran was sulking and vowed never to say anything ever again. 'You wait,' he thought. 'Tomorrow I'll race through my part in one minute flat. And then what are you going to do?'

**1** Identify the strengths and weaknesses of each member of the presentation team.

| Name | Strengths | Weaknesses |
|------|-----------|------------|
| **Gemma** | | |
| **Amaya** | | |
| **Adam** | | |
| **Imran** | | |

**2** What have the team done right, so far, in getting ready for their presentation?

**3** Why do you think they are having problems?

**4** If you were Gemma's tutor, what advice would you give her at this point?

## Activity: Preparing your presentation

You are asked to pitch a proposal for a children's television programme about either changing school, getting a puppy or kitten, or making a birthday cake. This programme should have an animated presenter. Your tutor is going to film the presentation.

You will be making the presentation using six PowerPoint slides as prompt cards. Use the spaces below to draft an overview of the content for each slide. These should provide, in turn, an outline of the programme's content, an explanation of why you are using an animated rather than human presenter, a description of your target audience, the personnel you will require for the production, details of the budget and, finally, a project schedule.

1

2

3

4

5

6

**TOP TIP**

When making a PowerPoint presentation, don't just read out what it says on the slides. The audience can do this. Use the slides as prompt cards.

# Step Ten: Maximise your opportunities and manage your problems

## Case study: Making the most of your opportunities

Leon made a really good start on his BTEC National and was really pleased with the grades he got for the first three assignments. It was during the second term of the course that things started to go wrong.

'I had a big row with my parents over the Christmas holidays and decided to move out. I couldn't afford a flat and ended up sleeping on a friend's couch. To pay for food I had to increase my shifts at the supermarket where I worked part-time, and I often ended up on the night shift stacking shelves. I found I got very tired, and without anyone around to insist I went to college I just bunked off.

'After about a month my friend started hassling me to get my own flat or to move back with my parents. Even with the supermarket job I couldn't afford my own place, and I realised that the argument with my parents had been pretty stupid anyway. I spoke to them and they agreed I could move back in as long as I started attending college.

'I was really worried as I hadn't attended for over three weeks and I knew that I'd missed a big chunk of a group filming project. I didn't think I'd be able to catch up, but I went to talk to the tutor about it.

'At first he seemed a bit annoyed that I hadn't been at college, but he really seemed to understand when I explained what had been going on. He gave me some notes on how I could catch up. I had missed too much of the group filming project, but he said there'd be other opportunities to get a grade in that unit.

'He also said that it would have been better if I'd spoken to the college when the problem first occurred, as there are a services that the college could have put me in touch with that might have helped with the problems I was having. I hope I don't have a problem like this again, but if I do, I'll know that at least there is someone I can talk to about it.'

### Reflection points

Do you know who you can talk to if you have a problem that you don't want your tutors to know about?

Do you know your college's guidelines for the late submission of work due to personal circumstances?

If you can't attend college for an extended period, how do you think your tutor might be able to help?

---

If your course takes one or two years to complete, then it is highly likely that you will experience some highs and lows in that time. You may find one or two topics harder than the rest. There may be distractions in your personal life to cope with, all of which mean than you may not always be able to do your best.

It is, therefore, sensible to have an action plan to help you cope. It's also wise to plan how to make the best of opportunities for additional experiences or learning. This section shows you how to do this.

### TOP TIP

Because life rarely runs smoothly, it's sensible to capitalise on the opportunities that come your way and have a plan to deal with problems.

# Making the most of your opportunities

There will be many opportunities for learning on your course, not all of which will be in school or college. You should prepare for some of the following to maximise the opportunities that each offer.

- **External visits**. Prepare in advance by reading about relevant topics. Make notes when you are there. Write up your notes neatly and file them safely for future reference.

- **Visiting speakers**. Questions can usually be submitted to the speaker in advance. Think carefully about information that you would find helpful. Make notes, unless someone has been appointed to make notes for the whole group. You may be asked to thank the speaker on behalf of your group.

- **Work experience**. If work experience is an essential part of your course, your tutor will help you to organise your placement and tell you about the evidence you need to obtain. You may also get a special logbook in which to record your experiences. Read and re-read the units to which your evidence will apply, and make sure you understand the grading criteria and what you need to obtain. Make time to write up your notes, logbook and/or diary every night (if possible), while everything is fresh in your mind.

- **In your own workplace**. If you have a full-time or part-time job, watch for opportunities to find out more about relevant topics that relate to your course, such as health and safety, teamwork, dealing with customers, IT security and communications. Your employer will have had to address all of these issues. Finding out more about these issues will broaden your knowledge and give more depth to your assessment responses.

- **Television, newspapers, podcasts and other information sources**. The media can be an invaluable source of information. Look out for news bulletins relating to your studies, as well as information in topical television programmes – from *The Apprentice* to *Top Gear*. You can also read news headlines online. Podcasts are useful, too. It will help if you know what topics you will be studying in the months to come, so you can spot useful opportunities as they arise.

## TOP TIP

Remember that you can use online catch-up services such as the BBC iPlayer or 4oD (for Channel 4 shows) to see TV programmes you have missed recently.

# Minimising problems

Hopefully, any problems you experience during your course will only be minor, such as struggling to find an acceptable working method with someone in your team.

You should already know who to talk to about these issues, and who to go to if that person is absent or you would prefer to talk to someone else. If your problems are affecting your work, it's sensible to see your tutor promptly. It is a rare learner who is enthusiastic about every topic and gets on well with everyone else doing the course, so your tutor won't be surprised and will give you useful guidance (in confidence) to help.

## TOP TIP

Don't delay talking to someone in confidence if you have a serious problem. If your course tutor is unavailable, talk to another staff member you like and trust.

## Other sources of help

If you are unfortunate enough to have a more serious personal problem, the following sources of help may be available in your centre.

- **Professional counselling.** There may be a professional counselling service. If you see a counsellor, nothing you say during the session can be mentioned to another member of staff without your permission.

- **Complaint procedures.** If you have a serious complaint, the first step is to talk to your tutor. If you can't resolve your problem informally, there will be a formal learner complaint procedure. These procedures are used only for serious issues, not for minor difficulties.

- **Appeals procedures.** If you disagree with your final grade for an assignment, check the grading criteria and ask the subject tutor to explain how the grade was awarded. If you are still unhappy, talk to your personal tutor. If you still disagree, you have the right to make a formal appeal.

- **Disciplinary procedures.** These exist for when learners consistently flout a centre's rules, and ensure that all learners are dealt with in the same way. Hopefully, you will never get into trouble, but you should make sure that you read these procedures carefully to see what could happen if you did. Remember that being honest and making a swift apology is always the wisest course of action.

- **Serious illness.** Whether this involves you, a family member or a close friend, it could affect your attendance. Discuss the problem with your tutor promptly; you will be missing information from the first day you are absent. There are many solutions in this type of situation – such as sending notes by post and updating you electronically (providing you are well enough to cope with the work).

### TOP TIP

It's important to know your centre's procedures for dealing with important issues such as complaints, major illnesses, learner appeals and disciplinary matters.

## Key points

- Don't miss opportunities to learn more about relevant topics through external visits, listening to visiting speakers, work experience, being at work or even watching television.

- If you have difficulties or concerns, talk to your tutor, or another appropriate person, promptly to make sure your work isn't affected.

### Action points

1 Prepare in advance to maximise your opportunities.
   a) List the opportunities available on your course for obtaining more information and talking to experts. You can check with your tutor to make sure you've identified them all.

   b) Check the content of each unit you will be studying so that you know the main topics and focus of each.

   c) Identify the information that may be relevant to your course on television, on radio, in newspapers and in podcasts.

2 Make sure you know how to cope if you have a serious problem.
   a) Check your centre's procedures so you know who to talk to in a crisis, and who to contact if that person is absent.

   b) Find out where you can get hold of a copy of the main procedures in your centre that might affect you if you have a serious problem. Then read them.

## Activity: Knowing what to do when you have a problem

Knowing how to react and where to go if you have a problem is really important.

How would you react to the these problems or issues? If you need to speak to a third party, then find out the people in your college or school with whom you can discuss problems confidentially.

| Issue or problem | How would you react? Where would you go for help? |
|---|---|
| You don't understand why you have been given a low grade for an assignment. | |
| You are struggling to meet the deadline for a piece of work. | |
| You need help completing a written piece of work. | |
| Other students on the course have specialist equipment, such as video cameras, that you can't afford to buy. | |
| You can't afford to travel to college. | |
| You know that one of the people on your course is being bullied by two other learners. | |
| You are studying on the Television and Film pathway but three weeks into the course you really think you should have chosen the Sound Recording pathway. | |

# AND FINALLY ...

Refer to this Study Skills Guide whenever you need to remind yourself about something related to your course. Keep it in a safe place so that you can use it whenever you need to refresh your memory. That way, you'll get the very best out of your course – and yourself!

## TOP TIP

The time and effort you will be putting into this course deserve to be rewarded. Make sure you know how to confront and successfully overcome problems.

# Skills building

This section has been written to help you improve the skills needed to do your best in your assignments. You may be excellent at some skills already, while others may need further work. The skills you can expect to demonstrate on your course include:

- your personal, learning and thinking skills (**PLTS**)
- your **functional skills** of ICT, maths/numeracy and English
- your proofreading and document production skills.

## Personal, learning and thinking skills (PLTS)

These are the skills, personal qualities and behaviour that enable you to operate more independently, work more confidently with other people and be more effective at work. You'll develop these on your BTEC Level 3 National course through a variety of experiences and as you take on different roles and responsibilities.

The skills are divided into six groups.

1 **Independent enquirers** can process and evaluate information they investigate from different perspectives. They can plan what to do and how to do it, and take into account the consequences of making different decisions.

2 **Creative thinkers** generate and explore different ideas. They make connections between ideas, events and experiences that enable them to be inventive and imaginative.

3 **Reflective learners** can assess themselves and other people. They can evaluate their own strengths and limitations. They set themselves realistic goals, monitor their own performance and welcome feedback.

4 **Team workers** collaborate with other people to achieve common goals. They are fair and considerate to others, whether as a team leader or team member, and take account of different opinions.

5 **Self-managers** are well-organised and show personal responsibility, initiative, creativity and enterprise. They look for new challenges and responsibilities, and are flexible when priorities change.

6 **Effective participators** play a full part in the life of their school, college, workplace or wider community by taking responsible action to bring improvements for others as well as themselves.

### Action points

1 Many parts of this Study Skills Guide relate to the development of your own personal, learning and thinking skills. For each of the following, suggest the main skill groups to which the chapter relates. Refer to the box above and write a number next to each chapter title below.

a) Use your time wisely. _____

b) Understand how to research and analyse information. _____

c) Work productively as a member of a group. _____

d) Understand yourself. _____

e) Utilise all your resources. _____

f) Maximise your opportunities and manage your problems. _____

**2** You have been on your BTEC National course for a few months now and, although everyone is enjoying the work, you realise that some of the learners have complaints.

First, several learners object to an increase in the price of printouts and photocopying, on the basis that they can't do good work for their assignments if this is too expensive. You disagree and think that the prices are reasonable, given the cost of paper.

Second, a timetable change means your 2 pm – 4 pm Friday afternoon class has been moved to 9 am – 11 am. Some learners are annoyed and want it changed back, while others are delighted.

**a)** For the first problem, identify four factors which could indicate that those complaining about the price rise might be justified.

1

2

3

4

**b)** Now consider the second problem.

**i)** Think about which learners in your group would be most affected by the timetable change. Who might be most disturbed? Who might benefit from the earlier start?

**ii)** Try to think of a creative solution, or compromise, that would please both groups.

**c)** During the discussions about these issues, some quieter members of the class are often shouted down by the more excitable members. Suggest a strategy for dealing with this which everyone is likely to accept.

You can also check your ideas with the suggestions given on page 107.

**3 a)** Complete the chart opposite, identifying occasions when you may need to demonstrate personal, learning and thinking skills in your future career. Alternatively, apply each area to a part-time job you are currently doing.

**b)** Identify areas where you think you are quite strong and put a tick in the 'S' column. Check that you could provide evidence to support this judgement, such as a time when you have demonstrated this skill.

**c)** Now consider areas where you are not so good and put a cross in the 'W' column.

**d)** Then practise self-management by identifying two appropriate goals to achieve over the next month, and make a note of them in the space provided. If possible, talk through your ideas at your next individual tutorial.

| Personal, learning and thinking skills for future career/current part-time job | | | | |
|---|---|---|---|---|
| **Skill group** | **Example skills** | **Occasions when you use/ will use skill** | **S** | **W** |
| Independent enquirers | Finding information<br><br>Solving problems<br><br>Making decisions<br><br>Reconciling conflicting information or views<br><br>Justifying decisions | | | |
| Creative thinkers | Finding imaginative solutions<br><br>Making original connections<br><br>Finding new ways to do something<br><br>Opportunities for being innovative and inventive | | | |
| Reflective learners | Goals you may set yourself<br><br>Reviewing your own progress<br><br>Encouraging feedback<br><br>Dealing with setbacks or criticism | | | |
| Team workers | Working with others<br><br>Coping with different views from your own<br><br>Adapting your behaviour<br><br>Being fair and considerate | | | |
| Self-managers | Being self-starting and showing initiative<br><br>Dealing positively with changing priorities<br><br>Organising your own time and resources<br><br>Dealing with pressure<br><br>Managing your emotions | | | |
| Effective participators | Identifying issues of concern to others<br><br>Proposing ways forward<br><br>Identifying improvements for others<br><br>Influencing other people<br><br>Putting forward a persuasive argument | | | |
| Goals | 1 | | | |
| | 2 | | | |

# Functional skills

Functional skills are practical skills that everyone needs to have in order to study and work effectively. They involve using and applying English, maths and ICT.

## Improving your literacy skills

### Your written English communication skills

A good vocabulary increases your ability to explain yourself clearly. Work that is presented without spelling and punctuation errors looks professional, and increases the likelihood of someone understanding your intended meaning. Your written communication skills will be tested in many assignments. You should work at improving areas of weakness, such as spelling, punctuation or vocabulary.

Try the following ideas to help you improve your written communication skills.

- Read more as this introduces you to new words, and it will help your spelling.

- Look up new words in a dictionary and try to use them in conversation.

- Use a thesaurus (you can access one electronically in Word) to find alternatives to words you use a lot; this adds variety to your work.

- Never use words you don't understand in the hope that they sound impressive.

- Write neatly, so people can read what you've written.

- Do crosswords to improve your word power and spelling.

- Improve your punctuation – especially the use of apostrophes – either by using an online programme or by using a communication textbook.

- Go to page 108 to find out how to gain access to some helpful websites.

### Verbal and non-verbal communication (NVC) skills

Talking appropriately means using the right words and 'tone'; using the right body language means sending positive signals to reinforce this message – such as smiling at someone when you say 'Hello'. Both verbal and non-verbal communication skills are essential when dealing with people at work.

The following ideas are some hints for successful communication.

- Be polite, tactful and sensitive to other people's feelings.

- Think about the words and phrases that you like to hear, and use them when communicating with other people.

- Use simple language so that people can understand you easily. Explain what you mean, when necessary.

- Speak at the right pace. Don't speak so slowly that everyone loses interest, or so fast that no one can understand you.

- Speak loudly enough for people to hear you clearly – but don't shout!

- Think about the specific needs of different people – whether you are talking to a senior manager, an important client, a shy colleague or an angry customer.

- Recognise the importance of non-verbal communication (NVC) so that you send positive signals by smiling, making eye contact, giving an encouraging nod or leaning forwards to show interest.

- Read other people's body language to spot if they are anxious or impatient so that you can react appropriately.

### TOP TIP

Make sure you use the right tone for the person you're talking to. Would you talk to an adult in the same way you'd talk to a very young child?

## Action points

**1** Go to page 108 to find out how to gain access to websites which can help you to improve your literacy skills.

**2** A battery made in China contained the following information.

> **DO NOT CONNECT IMPROPERLY**
>
> **CHARGE OR DISPOSE OF IN FIRE**

**a)** Can you see any problems with this? Give a reason for your answer.

_____

_____

_____

_____

_____

_____

**b)** Reword the information so that it is unambiguous.

_____

_____

_____

_____

**3** If you ever thought you could completely trust the spellchecker on your computer, type the text given in box A on the next page into your computer. Your spellchecker will not highlight a single error, yet even at a glance you should be able to spot dozens of errors!

Read the passage in box A and try to understand it. Then rewrite it in box B on the next page without spelling, grammatical or punctuation errors. Compare your finished work with the suggested version on page 107.

**Box A**

> Anyone desirable to write books or reports, be they short or long, should strive too maximise they're optimal use of one's English grammar and obliviously there is an need for correct spelling two one should not neglect punctuation neither.
>
> Frequent lea, many people and individuals become confusing or just do not no it, when righting, when words that mean different, when sounding identically, or when pronounced very similar, are knot too bee spelled inn the same whey. The quay two suck seeding is dew care, a lack off witch Leeds too Miss Spellings that mite otherwise of bean a voided. Spell chequers donut find awl missed takes.
>
> Despite all the pitfalls how ever, with practise, patients and the right altitude, any one can soon become a grate writer and speaker, as what I did.

**Box B** Now rewrite the passage in the space below without errors.

**4** In each of the statements listed in the table below suggest what the body language described might mean.

| Statement | What might this body language mean? |
|---|---|
| **a)** You are talking to your manager when he steps away from you and crosses his arms over his chest. | |
| **b)** You are talking to your friend about what she did at the weekend but she's avoiding making eye contact with you. | |
| **c)** During a tutorial session, your tutor is constantly tapping his fingers on the arm of his chair. | |
| **d)** Whenever you talk to your friend about your next assignment, she bites her lower lip. | |

# Improving your maths or numeracy skills

If you think numeracy isn't relevant to you, then think again! Numeracy is an essential life skill. If you can't carry out basic calculations accurately then you will have problems, perhaps when you least expect them. You'll often encounter numbers in various contexts – sometimes they will be correctly given, sometimes not. Unless you have a basic understanding about numeracy, you won't be able to tell the difference.

Good numeracy skills will improve your ability to express yourself, especially in assignments and at work. If you have problems, there are strategies that you can practise to help:

- Try to do basic calculations in your head, then check them on a calculator.

- Ask your tutor for help if important calculations give you problems.

- When you are using your computer, use the onscreen calculator (or a spreadsheet package) to do calculations.

- Investigate puzzle sites and brain training software, such as Dr Kageyama's Maths Training by Nintendo.

## Action points

1 Go to page 108 to find out how to gain access to websites which can help you to improve your numeracy skills.

2 Try the following task with a friend or family member.

Each of you should write down 36 simple calculations in a list, eg

$8 \times 6$, $19 - 8$, $14 + 6$.

Exchange lists. See who can answer the most calculations correctly in the shortest time.

3 Figures aren't always what they appear to be. For example, Sophie watches *Who Wants To Be a Millionaire?* She hears Chris Tarrant say

that there have been over 500 shows, with 1200 contestants who have each won over £50,000 on average. Five people have won £1 million.

Sophie says she is going to enter because she is almost certain to win more than £50,000 and could even win a million pounds.

a) On the figures given, what is the approximate total of money won over 500 shows (to the nearest £ million)?

b) Assuming that Sophie is chosen to appear on the show, and makes it on air as a contestant, do you think Sophie's argument that she will 'almost certainly' win more than £50,000 is correct? Give a reason for your answer.

(The correct answer is on page 107.)

4 You have a part-time job and have been asked to carry out a survey on the usage of the drinks vending machine. You decide to survey 500 people, and find that:

- 225 use the machine to buy one cup of coffee per day only

- 100 use the machine to buy one cup of tea per day only

- 75 use the machine to buy one cup of cold drink per day only

- 50 use the machine to buy one cup of hot chocolate per day only

- the rest are non-users

- the ratio of male to female users is 2:1.

a) How many men in your survey use the machine?

**b)** How many women in your survey use the machine?

**c)** Calculate the proportion of the people in your survey that use the machine.

Express this as a fraction and as a percentage.

**d)** What is the ratio of coffee drinkers to tea drinkers in your survey?

**e)** What is the ratio of coffee drinkers to hot chocolate drinkers in your survey?

**f)** If people continue to purchase from the machine in the same ratio found in your survey, and last month 1800 cups of coffee were sold, what would you expect the sales of the cold drinks to be?

**g)** Using the answer to f), if coffee costs 65p and all cold drinks cost 60p, how much would have been spent in total last month on these two items?

# Improving your ICT skills

Good ICT skills are an asset in many aspects of your daily life and not just for those studying to be IT practitioners.

These are ways in which you can improve your ICT skills.

- Check that you can use the main features of the software packages you need to produce your assignments, eg Word, Excel and PowerPoint.
- Choose a good search engine and learn to use it properly. Go to page 108 to find out how to access websites with more information.
- Developing and using your IT skills enables you to enhance your assignments. This may include learning how to import and export text and artwork from one package to another, taking digital photographs and inserting them into your work, and/or creating drawings or diagrams by using appropriate software.

## Action points

**1** Check your basic knowledge of IT terminology by identifying each of these items on your computer screen:

**a)** taskbar

**b)** toolbar

**c)** title bar

**d)** menu bar

**e)** mouse pointer

**f)** scroll bars

**g)** status bar

**h)** insertion point

**i)** maximise/ minimise button.

**2** Assess your IT skills by identifying the packages and operations you find easy to use and those that you find more difficult. If you use Microsoft Office products (Word, PowerPoint, Access or Excel) you can find out more about improving your skills online. Go to page 108 to find out how you can access a useful website for this action point.

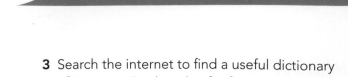

3 Search the internet to find a useful dictionary of IT terms. Bookmark it for future use. Find out the meaning of any of the following terms that you don't know already:

a) portal

b) cached link

c) home page

d) browser

e) firewall

f) HTML

g) URL

h) cookie

i) hyperlink

j) freeware.

## Proofreading and document preparation skills

Improving your keyboard, document production and general IT skills can save you hours of time. When you have good skills, the work you produce will be of a far more professional standard.

- Think about learning to touch-type. Your centre may have a workshop you can join, or you can use an online program – go to page 108 to find out how you can access websites that will allow you to test and work on improving your typing skills.

- Obtain correct examples of any document formats you will have to use, such as a report or summary, either from your tutor, the internet or from a textbook.

- Proofread all your work carefully. A spellchecker won't find all your mistakes, so you must read through it yourself as well.

- Make sure your work looks professional by using a suitable typeface and font size, as well as reasonable margins.

- Print your work and store the printouts neatly, so that it stays in perfect condition for when you hand it in.

## Action points

1 You can check and improve your typing skills using online typing sites – see link in previous section.

2 Check your ability to create documents by scoring yourself out of 5 for each of the following questions, where 5 is something you can do easily and 0 is something you can't do at all. Then focus on improving every score where you rated yourself 3 or less.

I know how to:

a) create a new document and open a saved document _____

b) use the mouse to click, double-click and drag objects _____

c) use drop-down menus _____

d) customise my toolbars by adding or deleting options _____

e) save and/or print a document _____

f) create folders and sub-folders to organise my work _____

g) move a folder I use regularly to My Places _____

h) amend text in a document _____

i) select, copy, paste and delete information in a document _____

j) quickly find and replace text in a document _____

k) insert special characters _____

l) create a table or insert a diagram in a document _____

m) change the text size, font and colour _____

n) add bold, italics or underscore _____

o) create a bullet or numbered list _____

p) align text left, right or centred _____

q) format pages before they are printed _____

r) proofread a document so that there are no mistakes _____.

# Answers

## Activity: Let's give you a tip... (page 79)

a) i) Fact
   ii) Opinion – the number cannot be validated
   iii) Fact
   iv) Opinion
   v) Opinion
   vi) Opinion – again, the number is estimated

# Skills building answers

## PLTS action points (page 98)

1 a) Use your time wisely = **5** Self-managers
   b) Understand how to research and analyse information = **1** Independent enquirers, **5** Self-managers
   c) Work productively as a member of a group = **4** Team workers, **6** Effective participators
   d) Understand yourself = **3** Reflective learners
   e) Utilise all your resources = **5** Self-managers
   f) Maximise your opportunities and manage your problems – **1** Independent enquirers, **2** Creative thinkers, **3** Reflective learners, **5** Self-managers

2 a) Factors to consider in relation to the increased photocopying/printing charges include: the comparative prices charged by other schools/colleges, how often there is a price rise, whether any printing or photocopying at all can be done without charge, whether there are any concessions for special tasks or assignments, the availability of class sets of books/popular library books for loan (which reduces the need for photocopying).

b) i) An earlier start will be more likely to negatively affect those who live further away and who are reliant on public transport, particularly in rural areas. The earlier finish will benefit anyone who has a part-time job that starts on a Friday afternoon or who has after-college commitments, such as looking after younger sisters or brothers.

ii) The scope for compromise would depend on whether there are any classes between 11 am and 2 pm on a Friday, whether tutors had any flexibility, and whether the new 9 am – 11 am class could be moved to another time or day.

c) One strategy would be to allow discussion for a set time, ensure everyone had spoken, then put the issue to a vote. The leader should prompt suggestions from quieter members by asking people individually what they think.

## Literacy skills action points (page 101)

2 a) The statement reads as if it is acceptable to either charge it or dispose of it in fire.
   b) Do not connect this battery improperly. Do not recharge it and do not dispose of it in fire.

3 Anyone who wishes to write books or reports, whether short or long, should try to use English grammatically. Obviously there is a need for correct spelling, too. Punctuation should also not be neglected.

Frequently, people confuse words with different meanings when they are writing, especially when these sound identical or very similar, even when they must not be spelled in the same way. The key to succeeding is due care, a lack of which leads to misspellings that might otherwise have been avoided. Spellcheckers do not find all mistakes.

Despite all the pitfalls, however, with practice, patience and the right attitude, anyone can soon become a great writer and speaker, like me.

4 Possible answers.

   **a)** Stepping backwards and crossing arms across the chest might indicate that you manager is creating a barrier between you and himself. This may be because he is angry with you.

   **b)** Your friend may be feeling guilty about what she did at the weekend, or not confident that you will approve of what she tells you.

   **c)** Your tutor might be frustrated as he has many things to do and so wants the tutorial to finish quickly.

   **d)** Your friend might be anxious about the next assignment or about the time she has to complete it.

## Numeracy action points (page 104)

3 **a)** £60 million

   **b)** Sophie's argument is incorrect as £50,000 is an average, ie some contestants will win more, but many will win much less. The distribution of prize money is greater at lower amounts because more people win small amounts of money than large amounts – and only five contestants have won the top prize of £1 million.

4 **a)** 300

   **b)** 150

   **c)** 9/10ths, 90%

   **d)** 225:100 (= 45:20) = 9:4

   **e)** 225:50 = 9:2

   **f)** 600

   **g)** £1530

# Accessing website links

Links to various websites are referred to throughout this BTEC Level 3 National Study Skills Guide. To ensure that these links are up to date, that they work and that the sites aren't inadvertently linked to any material that could be considered offensive, we have made the links available on our website: www.pearsonhotlinks.co.uk. When you visit the site, search for either the title BTEC Level 3 National Study Skills Guide in Creative Media Production or ISBN 9781846905568. From here you can gain access to the website links and information on how they can be used to help you with your studies.

# Useful terms

### Accreditation of Prior Learning (APL)
Some of your previous achievements and experiences may be able to be used to count towards your qualification.

### Apprenticeships
Schemes that enable you to work and earn money at the same time as you gain further qualifications (an NVQ award and a technical certificate) and improve your functional skills. Apprentices learn work-based skills relevant to their job role and their chosen industry. See page 108 to find out how to access a useful website where you can find out more.

### Assessment methods
Techniques used to check that your work demonstrates the learning and understanding required for your qualification, such as assignments, case studies and practical tasks.

### Assessor
An assessor is the tutor who marks or assesses your work.

### Assignment
A complex task or mini-project set to meet specific grading criteria and learning outcomes.

### Awarding body
An organisation responsible for devising, assessing and issuing qualifications. The awarding body for all BTEC qualifications is Edexcel.

### Credit value
The number of credits attached to your BTEC course. The credit value increases in relation to the length of time you need to complete the course, from 30 credits for a BTEC Level 3 Certificate, 60 credits for a Subsidiary Diploma, 120 credits for a Diploma, and up to 180 credits for an Extended Diploma.

### Degrees
Higher education qualifications offered by universities and colleges. Foundation degrees take two years to complete; honours degrees may take three years or longer.

### Department for Business Innovation and Skills (BIS)
BIS is responsible for further and higher education and skills training, as well as functions related to trade and industry. See page 108 to find out how to access a useful website where you can find out more.

### Department for Education
The Department for Education is responsible for schools and education, as well as for children's services. See page 108 to find out how to access a useful website where you can find out more.

### Distance learning
When you learn and/or study for a qualification at home or at work. You communicate with your tutor and/or the centre that organises the course by post, telephone or electronically.

### Educational Maintenance Award (EMA)
An EMA is a means-tested award that provides eligible learners under 19 who are studying a full-time course at school or college with a cash sum of money every week. See page 108 to find out how to access a useful website where you can find out more.

### External verification
Formal checking of the programme by an Edexcel representative that focuses on sampling various assignments to check content, accurate assessment and grading.

### Forbidden combinations
There are some qualifications that cannot be taken simultaneously because their content is too similar.

### Functional skills
Practical skills in English, maths and ICT that enable people to work confidently, effectively and independently. Level 2 Functional Skills are mapped to the units of BTEC Level 3 National qualifications. They aren't compulsory to achieve on the course, but are of great use.

### Grade boundaries
Pre-set points that determine whether you will achieve a pass, merit or distinction as the overall final grade(s) for your qualification.

### Grading criteria
The specific evidence you have to demonstrate to obtain a particular grade in the unit.

### Grading domains

The main areas of learning that support the learning outcomes. On a BTEC Level 3 National course these are: application of knowledge and understanding; development of practical and technical skills; personal development for occupational roles; application of PLTS and functional skills.

### Grading grid

The table in each unit of your qualification specification that sets out what you have to show you can do.

### Higher education (HE)

Post-secondary and post-further education, usually provided by universities and colleges.

### Higher-level skills

These are skills such as evaluating or critically assessing information. They are more difficult than lower-level skills such as writing a description or making a list. You must be able to demonstrate higher-level skills to achieve a distinction.

### Indicative reading

Recommended books and journals whose content is both suitable and relevant for the BTEC unit studied.

### Induction

A short programme of events at the start of a course designed to give you essential information and introduce you to your fellow learners and tutors, so that you can settle down as quickly and easily as possible.

### Internal verification

The quality checks carried out by nominated tutors at your school or college to ensure that all assignments are at the right level and cover appropriate learning outcomes and grading criteria, and that all assessors are marking work consistently and to the same standard.

### Investors in People (IiP)

A national quality standard that sets a level of good practice for training and developing of people within a business. Participating organisations must demonstrate commitment to achieving the standard.

### Learning outcomes

The knowledge and skills you must demonstrate to show that you have effectively learned a unit.

### Learning support

Additional help that is available to all learners in a school or college who have learning difficulties or other special needs.

### Levels of study

The depth, breadth and complexity of knowledge, understanding and skills required to achieve a qualification, which also determines its level. Level 2 equates to GCSE level and Level 3 equates to A-level. As you successfully achieve one level, you can then progress to the next. BTEC qualifications are offered at Entry Level, then Levels 1, 2, 3, 4 and 5.

### Local Education Authority (LEA)

The local government body responsible for providing education for all learners of compulsory school age. The LEA is also responsible for managing the education budget for 16–19-year-old learners in its area.

### Mandatory units

These are units that all learners must complete to gain a qualification, in this case a BTEC Level 3 National. Some BTEC qualifications have an over arching title, eg Construction, but within Construction you can choose different pathways. Your chosen pathway may have additional mandatory units specific to that pathway.

### Mentor

A more experienced person who will guide you and counsel you if you have a problem or difficulty.

### Mode of delivery

The way in which a qualification is offered to learners, for example, part-time, full-time, as a short course or by distance learning.

### National Occupational Standard (NOS)

Statements of the skills, knowledge and understanding you need to develop in order to be competent at a particular job.

### National Vocational Qualification (NVQ)

Qualifications that concentrate on the practical skills and knowledge required to do a job competently. They are usually assessed in the workplace and range from Level 1 (the lowest) to Level 5 (the highest).

### Nested qualifications

Qualifications that have 'common' units, so that learners can easily progress from one to another by adding on more units

## Ofqual
The public body responsible for regulating qualifications, exams and tests in England.

## Optional units
Units on your course from which you may be able to make a choice. They help you specialise your skills, knowledge and understanding, and may help progression into work or further education.

## Pathway
All BTEC Level 3 National qualifications comprise a small number of mandatory units and a larger number of optional units. These units are grouped into different combinations to provide alternative pathways to achieving the qualification. These pathways are usually linked to different career preferences.

## Peer review
This involves feedback on your performance by your peers (members of your team or class group.) You will also be given an opportunity to review their performance.

## Plagiarism
The practice of copying someone else's work, or work from any other sources (eg the internet), and passing it off as your own. This practice is strictly forbidden on all courses.

## Personal, learning and thinking skills (PLTS)
The skills, personal qualities and behaviour that improve your ability to work independently. Developing these skills makes you more effective and confident at work. Opportunities for developing these skills are a feature of all BTEC Level 3 National courses. These skills aren't compulsory to achieve on the course, but are of great use to you.

## Portfolio
A collection of work compiled by a learner, usually as evidence of learning, to present to an assessor.

## Procrastinator
Someone who is forever putting off or delaying work, either because they are lazy or because they have poor organisational skills.

## Professional body
An organisation that exists to promote or support a particular profession, for example the Royal Institute of British Architects (RIBA).

## Professional development and training
This involves undertaking activities relevant to your job to increase and/or update your knowledge and skills.

## Project
A project is a comprehensive piece of work, which normally involves original research and investigation by an individual or by a team. The findings and results may be presented in writing and summarised as a presentation.

## Qualifications and Credit Framework (QCF)
The QCF is a framework for recognising skills and qualifications. It does this by awarding credit for qualifications and units so that they are easier to measure and compare. All BTEC Level 3 National qualifications are part of the QCF.

## Qualifications and Curriculum Development Authority (QCDA)
The QCDA is responsible for maintaining and developing the national curriculum, delivering assessments, tests and examinations, and reforming qualifications.

## Quality assurance
In education, this is the process of continually checking that a course of study is meeting the specific requirements set down by the awarding body.

## Sector Skills Councils (SSCs)
The 25 employer-led, independent organisations responsible for improving workforce skills in the UK by identifying skill gaps and improving learning in the workplace. Each council covers a different type of industry.

## Semester
Many universities and colleges divide their academic year into two halves or semesters, one from September to January and one from February to July.

## Seminar
A learning event involving a group of learners and a tutor, which may be learner-led and follow research into a topic that has been introduced at an earlier stage.

## Study buddy
A person in your group or class who takes notes for you and keeps you informed of important developments if you are absent. You do the same for them in return.

### Time-constrained assignment
An assessment you must complete within a fixed time limit.

### Tutorial
An individual or small group meeting with your tutor at which you can discuss your current work and other more general course issues. At an individual tutorial, your progress on the course will be discussed, and you can raise any concerns or personal worries you may have.

### The University and Colleges Admissions Service (UCAS)
UCAS (pronounced 'you-cass') is the central organisation that processes all applications for higher education (HE) courses.

### UCAS points
The number of points allocated by UCAS for the qualifications you have obtained. Higher education institutions specify how many points you need to be accepted on the courses they offer. See page 108 to find out how to access a useful website where you can find out more.

### Unit abstract
The summary at the start of each BTEC unit that tells you what the unit is about.

### Unit content
Details about the topics covered by the unit and the knowledge and skills you need to complete it.

### Unit points
The number of points you gain when you complete a unit. These will depend on the grade you achieve (pass, merit or distinction).

### Vocational qualification
Designed to develop knowledge and understanding relevant to a chosen area of work.

### Work experience
Time you spend on an employer's premises when you learn about the enterprise, carry out work-based tasks and develop skills and knowledge.

Please note that all information given within these useful terms was correct at the time of going to print.